2 Hyperlink

Student Book

Albina Escobar

Acesse o conteúdo digital em **www.pearson.com.br/hyperlink2e**
Código de acesso: **728.157.817.512**

2ª Edição – São Paulo – 2014

Pearson

Diretor editorial e de conteúdo	Roger Trimer
Gerente editorial	Kelly Tavares
Coordenadora editorial	Veronica Teodorov
Editores de desenvolvimento	Renato Malkov, João Fittipaldi
Editor de campo	Allan Cravo
Editora de mídia e desenvolvimento	Mirian Navarro
Editor assistente	Mauricio Shiroma
Editor de produção	Gustavo Reis
Assistente de arte	Lucas Medeiros
Assistente editorial	Carolina Bostigo
Editora de iconografia	Maiti Salla
Assistentes de iconografia e licenciamento de texto	Cristiane Gameiro, Rebeca Fiamozzini
Preparação de texto	Mário Vilela
Ilustração	Kleber Moraes
Criações especiais	Vendo Editorial, Estúdio Sintonia
Projeto gráfico e capa	Pedro Gentile
Editoração eletrônica	Figurattiva Editorial
Fotos da capa	GettyImages
Produção de áudio	Maximal Studio
Manual do professor	Renato Malkov, Elaine C. C. Hodgson

Créditos das imagens: p. 9 Mikhail Bakunovich / Shutterstock; p. 10 TIMUR EMEK / AFP; p. 15 a Swinner / Shutterstock, b CandyBox Images / Shutterstock; p. 16 a iStockphoto /Thinkstock / Getty Images, b Hemera / Thinkstock / Getty Images, c Creatas / Thinkstock / Getty Images; d Comstock / Thinkstock / Getty Images, e iStockphoto /Thinkstock / Getty Images, f Hemera / Thinkstock / Getty Images; p. 18 a View Pictures/ Getty Images, b Marcio Jose Bastos Silva / Shutterstock, c Delmi Alvarez / Zuma Press / Corbis / Latinstock, d Stan Honda / AFP; p. 21 a Chad Baker / Ryan McVay / Digital Vision / Thinkstock, b S.Borisov / Shutterstock; p. 22 a Nasonov / Shutterstock, b iStockphoto / Thinkstock / Getty Images, c Ingo Schulz / imagebrok / Keystone, d Mtkang / Shutterstock; p. 27 a JUNG YEON-JE / AFP, b Goodshoot / Thinkstock / Getty Images, c Andrey_Popov / Shutterstock, d iStockphoto / Thinkstock / Getty Images, e Banana Stock / Thinkstock / Getty Images; p. 28 a Digital Vision / Thinkstock / GettyImages, b Alexander Kirch / Shutterstock, p. 30 a iStockphoto / Thinkstock / Getty Images, b Elder Vieira Salles / Shutterstock, c Andrea Dal Max / Shutterstock, d Marcello Lourenço / Tyba; p. 32 a Hemera / PhotoObjects / Thinkstock / Getty Images, b Akg-Images / Latinstock, c Sergio Stakhnyk / Shutterstock, d Science Museum / SSPL / Getty Images, e Dtopal / Shutterstock; p. 33 a Anna Kari / In Pictures / Corbis / Latinstock, b Andresr / Shutterstock, c Holger Leue / Look / LatinStock, d Tony Magdaraog / Shutterstock, e EML / Shutterstock; p. 34 a Stockbyte / Thinkstock / Getty Images, b Inside /AGE Fotostock / Grupo Keystone; p. 35 Clive Chilvers / Shutterstock; p. 39 a William Perugini / Shutterstock, b Danilo Verpa / Folhapress, c Photodisc / Thinkstock / Getty Images; p. 40 Monkey Business Images / Shutterstock; p. 41 a Dubova / Shutterstock, b Hemera / Thinkstock / Getty Images; p. 42 Julien M. Hekimian / Getty Images / AFP; p. 45 iStockphoto / Thinkstock / Getty Images; p. 46 a iStockphoto / Thinkstock / Getty Images, b Stockbyte / Thinkstock / Getty Images, c Nixx Photography / Shutterstock, d Roman Sigaev / Shutterstock, e Hainaultphoto / Shutterstock, f Leungchopan / Shutterstock, g Mikhail Zahranichny / Shutterstock, h iStockphoto / Thinkstock / Getty Images; p. 51 iStockphoto / Thinkstock / Getty Images; p. 52 RJ Lerich / Shutterstock; p. 54 a Bettmann / Corbis / Latinstock, b Selfiy / Shutterstock, c David H.Seymour / Shutterstock, d Featureflash / Shutterstock, e Topham Picturepoint / Top Foto / Keystone, f iStockphoto / Thinksotk / Getty Images; p. 55 iStockphoto / Thinksotk / Getty Images; p. 56 a Peter Gudella / Shutterstock, b Andrea Michele Piacquadio / Shutterstock, c Dmitry Vinogradov / Shutterstock, d Dmitry Naumov / Shutterstock, e iStockphoto / Thinksotk / Getty Images, f Creatas / Thinksotk / Getty Images, g Arjuna Kodisinghe / Shutterstock, h Bikeriderlondon / Shutterstock; p. 57 Nils Volkmer / Shutterstock; p. 58 a Morphart Creation / Shutterstock, b Tischenko Irina / Shutterstock, c White House Washington, D.C., United States, d Arogant / Shutterstock, e David Ross / Shutterstock, f Comstock / Thinkstock / Getty Images; p. 63 Jaren Jai Wicklund / Shutterstock; p. 64 a iStockphoto / Thinkstock / Getty Images, b Photodisc / Thinkstock / Getty Images, c Lifesize / ThinkStock / Getty Images, d iStockphoto / Thinkstock / Getty Images, e Suprijono Suharjoto / Thinkstock / Getty Images, f Arena Creative / Thinkstock / Getty Images, g Monkey Business Images / Shutterstock, h Yuri Arcurs / Shutterstock; p. 65 a Sergey Karpov / Shutterstock, b Les and Dave Jacobs / Glowimages, c Jaimie Duplass / Shutterstock, d Fred Fokkelman / Shutterstock, e Lissandra Melo / Shutterstock, f Ssuaphotos / Shutterstock, g Eans / Shutterstock, h iStockphoto / Thinkstock / Getty Images, i iStockphoto / Thinkstock / Getty Images, j Ilya Andriyanov / Shutterstock, k Picsfive / Shutterstock, l US Army / Photo Researchers / Getty Images, m Ozaiachin / Shutterstock; p. 66 a National Museum / The National Museum of Fine Arts, b National Museum in Warsaw, c Tretyakov Gallery, Moscow; p. 67 Stockbyte / Thinkstock / Getty Images; p. 69 Tanik / Shutterstock; p. 70 Hemera / Thinkstock / Getty Images; p. 77 Library of Congress; p. 78 a Heritage House Publishing, b Major Matthews collection; p. 81 Hemera / Thinkstock / Getty Images; p. 83 a Patrick Bergstrom - I Chose to Live, b Kntoh / Shutterstock; p. 88 Jagoda / Shutterstock; p. 89 a Konstanttin / Shutterstock, b Jupiterimages / Creatas / Thinkstock / Getty Images; p. 90 iStockphoto / Thinksotk / Getty Images; p. 91 Boris Sosnovyy / Shutterstock; p. 93 iStockphoto / Thinksotk / Getty Images; p. 94 XAOC / Shutterstock; p. 95 Pinkkoala / Shutterstock; p. 101 Sursad / Shutterstock; p. 102 a Humannet / Shutterstock, b Deklofenak / Shutterstock; p. 103 a Alena Brozova / Shutterstock, b Auremar / Shutterstock

Dados Internacionais de Catalogação na Publicação (CIP)
(Câmara Brasileira do Livro, SP, Brasil)

Escobar, Albina
Hyperlink : student book, 2 / Albina Escobar. --
2. ed. -- São Paulo : Pearson Education do Brasil, 2014.
ISBN 978-85-8143-901-3
1. Inglês (Ensino médio) I. Título.

13-07792 CDD-420.7

Índices para catálogo sistemático:
1. Inglês : Ensino médio 420.7

ISBN 978-85-8143-901-3	Hyperlink 2 Student Book - 2a ed
ISBN 978-85-430-0045-9	Hyperlink 2 Student Book with eText - 2a ed
ISBN 978-85-8143-918-1	Hyperlink 2 Student Book with MyEnglishLab - 2a ed
ISBN 978-85-8143-907-5	Hyperlink 2 Teacher Book - 2a ed

Pearson Education do Brasil Ltda.,
uma empresa do grupo Pearson Education
Rua Nélson Francisco, 26 – CEP: 02712-100 – São Paulo, SP – Brasil

10 9 8 7 6 5 4 Outubro/2015

CONTENTS

Caro aluno,

A língua inglesa é um conhecimento que não se encerra em si mesmo, mas abre portas para novas descobertas. O livro que tem em mãos irá ajudá-lo nesse processo de descobertas. Observe como aproveitar seu livro ao máximo.

LINK 6

LOG IN

1 Do you believe in legends?

2 Do you know of any Brazilian legends?

WORD BANK

crew: tripulação
cursed: amaldiçoada
devil: diabo
gale: vento muito violento
legend: lenda
rigging: cordame
uncanny: estranho

NOTES

Legend of The Flying Dutchman

By James Donahue

[...]

This ghost story has its origins in both Dutch and German legend. The most common is a tale about a Captain Hendrick Vanderdecken, who set sail in 1680 from Amsterdam to Batavia, in the Dutch East Indies, and disappeared in a gale while rounding the Cape [of Good Hope].

It is said that Vanderdecken ignored the danger and pressed on into the teeth of the tempest. The ship foundered, sending all aboard to their deaths. As punishment for his foolishness, Vanderdecken and his ship are doomed to spend eternity fighting the tempest at the Cape.

[...] There is a second version of the story. This one tells of a Captain Bernard Fokke, who was known for the uncanny speed of his trips from Holland to Java, and people said he was in league with the devil.

[...] In all of the stories, the ship remains unnamed. The reference to the "Flying Dutchman" appears to describe the cursed captain and not the ship.

According to most versions, the captain refuses to retreat in the face of the storm. In yet other stories, some terrible crime occurs on the ship, or the crew is struck by the plague and is not allowed to enter any port. For whatever the reason, the ship and its crew are doomed to sail forever.

[...] While there is general agreement that the Lost Dutchman is merely a legend, there have been actual reported sightings of a 17th-century sailing ship battling the elements at the Cape of Good Hope over the years.

Perhaps the first officially reported sighting occurred in 1835, when a crew of a British ship was rounding the cape and observed a "phantom ship" approaching in the shroud of a severe storm. The British crew said the vessel appeared to be on a collision course, but then it suddenly vanished.

The H.M.S. Bacchante encountered the Flying Dutchman again in 1881, also at the cape. The following day, one of the two men that made the sighting fell to his death from the rigging, thus enhancing the story to include a curse on those that see the ghostly vessel.

A more recent sighting was made by people on the shore in March, 1939. What was astounding was that it was seen by dozens of people who all gave a detailed description of a Dutch merchantman from the 17th century.

The last recorded sighting occurred at Cape Town in 1942, when four witnesses saw a sailing ship enter Table Bay and then disappear before their eyes.

Extracted from: http://perdurabo10.tripod.com/ships/id19.html

62 63

TEXT

Cada unidade é iniciada com um texto sobre temas atuais e diversos. O **Log In** levanta questões para você considerar e discutir antes da leitura e o **Word Bank** apresenta palavras cruciais para a compreensão de cada texto.

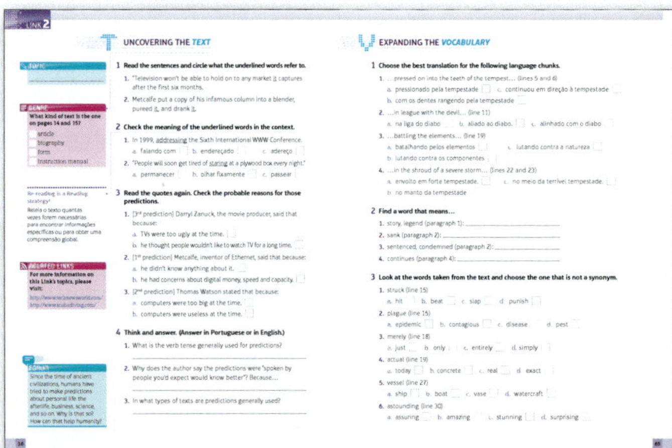

EXPANDING THE VOCABULARY

Essa seção oferece uma oportunidade para que você aumente seu vocabulário, analisando e trabalhando com as palavras apresentadas no texto.

UNCOVERING THE TEXT

Aqui você aprofunda seu entendimento do texto, explorando diferentes gêneros e respondendo a perguntas de compreensão e interpretação. Você também encontra aqui links para websites que se aprofundam nos temas explorados.

DISCOVERING GRAMMAR

Um atalho para a mecânica da língua inglesa é o que você encontra aqui. A cada unidade você tem a chance de explorar tópicos gramaticais, desenvolvendo o domínio formal do inglês.

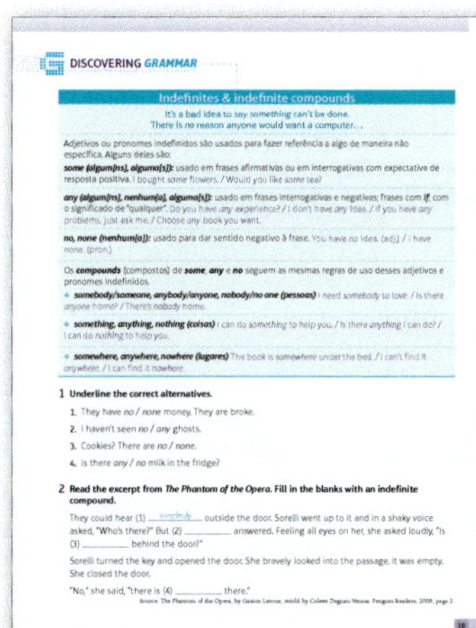

COMMUNICATION BYTES

O foco dessa seção é a comunicação oral genuína sobre assuntos relevantes. Aqui você se prepara para expressar suas próprias ideias e opiniões, explorando modelos e informações necessárias para o desenvolvimento de diálogos.

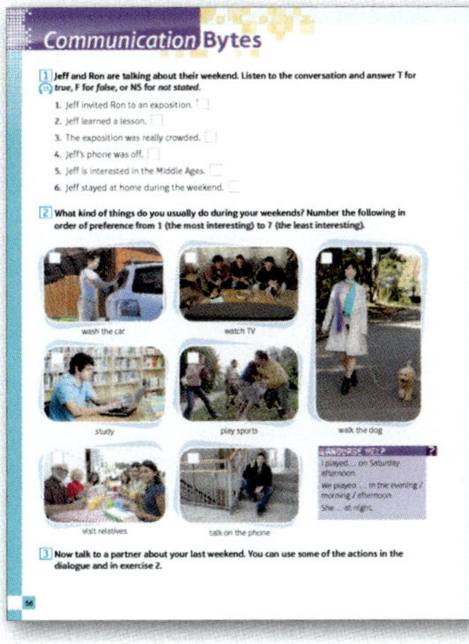

WRITING BITS

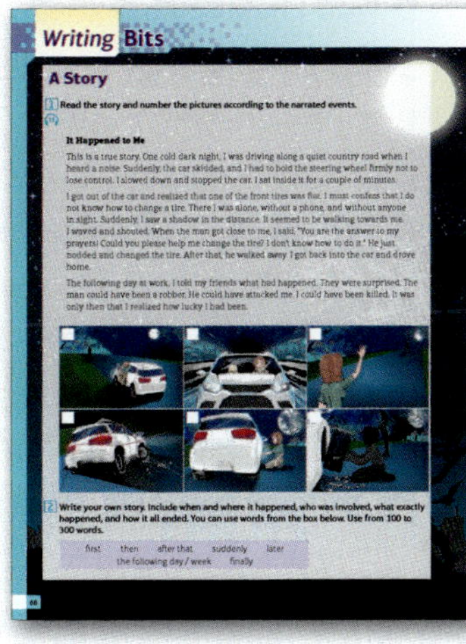

A produção escrita é o tema central aqui. Cada unidade lhe apresenta uma proposta de criação de texto, explorando gêneros variados e oferecendo modelos de diferentes estruturas textuais.

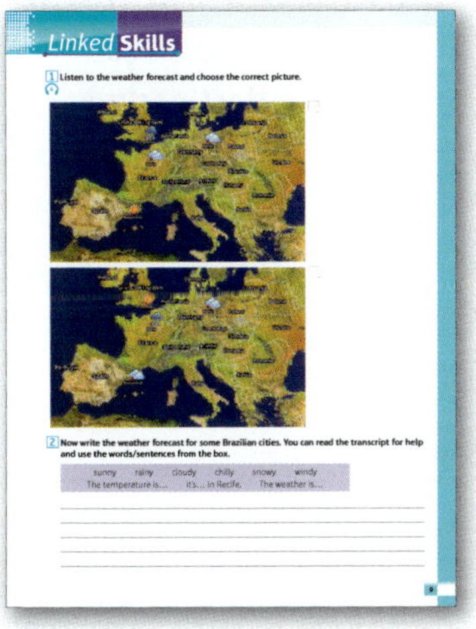

LINKED SKILLS

Aqui combinamos a habilidade de escuta com as outras aptidões. Você encontra nessa seção uma chance de conectar o texto falado ao escrito, ouvindo inglês falado com fluência e respondendo (de forma oral e escrita) às ideias apresentadas.

REVIEW

Para checar seu entendimento, e para que o conteúdo estudado seja ainda melhor fixado,

a cada duas unidades você encontra uma revisão, com exercícios que retomam os tópicos explorados.

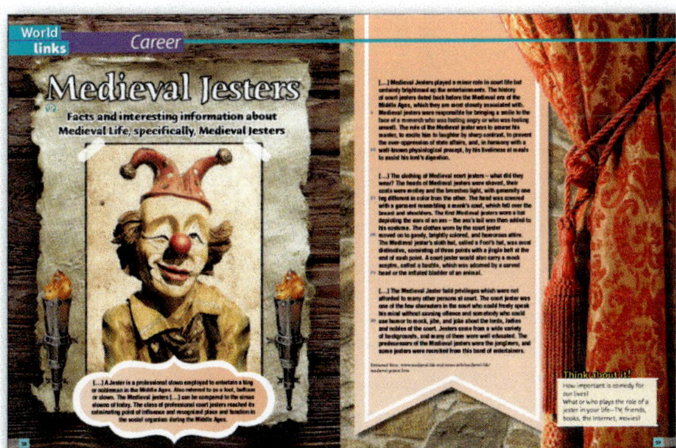

WORLD LINKS

Expandir as temáticas propostas pelos textos presentes em cada unidade é a proposta dessa seção. Você é convidado a repensar sua posição em relação ao mundo atual e as relações que nele desenvolvemos.

SO FAR, SO GOOD?

Aqui você reflete sobre seu aprendizado, baseado na análise pessoal do seu desempenho.

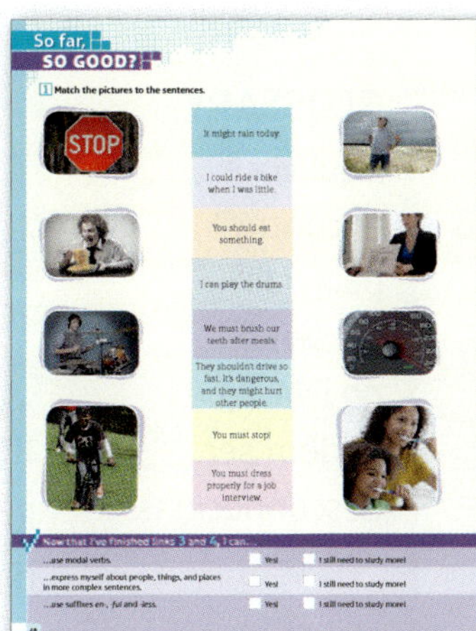

Primeiro você participa de uma atividade lúdica, depois avalia o próprio entendimento dos temas trabalhados.

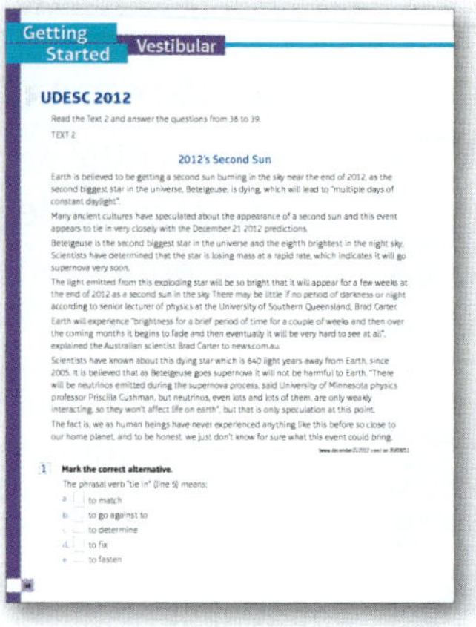

GETTING STARTED: VESTIBULAR

A possibilidade de aplicar seu conhecimento a questões extraídas de provas de vestibular é o que se apresenta nessa seção. Aqui você pode testar seu domínio da língua inglesa e familiarizar-se com o conteúdo avaliado em vestibulares de renomadas universidades.

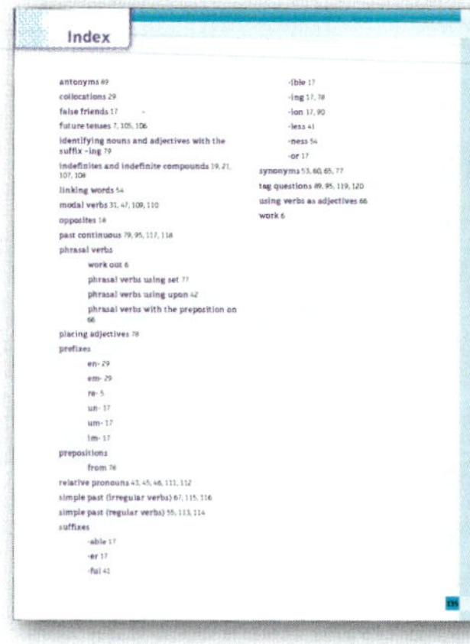

INDEX

Aqui você encontra tópicos gramaticais e de vocabulário organizados de maneira compilada.

GRAMMAR

Essa seção oferece a possibilidade de praticar mais a fundo os tópicos gramaticais apresentados no livro, resolvendo exercícios focados nos referidos tópicos.

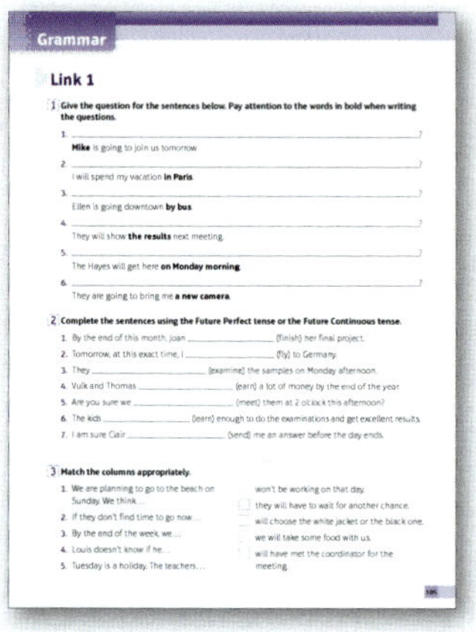

VOCABULARY LOG

Esse espaço é destinado à criação de um glossário pessoal, com vocabulário que você julgue importante.

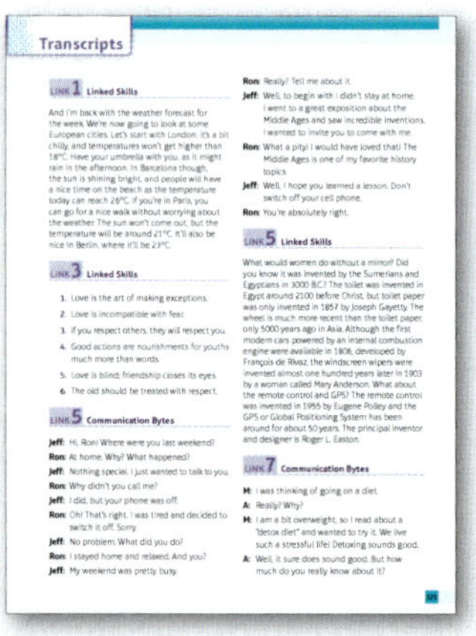

TRANSCRIPTS

Você pode consultar aqui as transcrições dos textos de áudio apresentados no livro.

REFERENCES

Essa seção oferece oportunidades para que você explore vídeos, websites e outros livros que expandem os temas trabalhados nas unidades apresentadas aqui.

GLOSSARY

Aqui você encontra palavras presentes no livro que podem ser desconhecidas.

IRREGULAR VERBS

Encontre aqui uma lista de verbos irregulares para sua referência.

Hyperlinks

future + predictions

LINK 1

A Carbon-Free, Stackable Rental Car

Communication Bytes

Linked Skills

World Links

LINK 2

Use it better: the worst tech predictions of all time

LINK 1

LOG IN

1 Take a quick look at the text. What is it about?

2 In your opinion, is it possible to control the problems of traffic and pollution?

WORD BANK

foldable: dobrável
linchpin: aspecto mais importante
low-cost: de baixo custo
provide: fornecer
rent: alugar
stackable: empilhável
slated: programado
unveil: mostrar pela primeira vez

NOTES

A Carbon-Free, Stackable Rental Car

An MIT group hopes that its foldable electric vehicles will cut pollution, and ease congestion.

The Smart Cities group at the MIT Media Lab is working on two low-cost electric vehicles that it hopes will revolutionize mass transit and help alleviate pollution. Next week, the group will unveil a prototype of its foldable electric scooter at the EICMA Motorcycle Show, in Milan. A prototype for the team's foldable electric car, called the City Car, is slated to follow next year.

The MIT group sees the vehicles as the linchpin in a strategy that aims to mitigate pollution with electric power, expand limited public space by folding and stacking vehicles like shopping carts, and alleviate congestion by letting people rent and return the vehicles to racks located near transportation hubs, such as train stations, airports, and bus depots.

"We're looking at urban personal mobility in a much more sustainable way than the private automobile provides," says William Mitchell, director of the Smart Cities research group.

MICHAEL PATRICK GIBSON
Thursday, November 1, 2007.

Extracted from: http://www.technologyreview.com/news/408982/a-carbon-free-stackable-rental-car/

UNCOVERING THE *TEXT*

TOPIC

____

GENRE

What kind of text is the one on page 3?

- ☐ article
- ☐ biography
- ☐ form
- ☐ instruction manual

1 Scan the text and find the following information.

1. Who's the director of the Smart Cities research group?

   ____
2. Where in Europe will the prototype of a scooter be unveiled?

   ____
3. What transportation hubs are mentioned in the text?

   ____
4. What's the City Car?

   ____

Scanning is a reading strategy!

É quando passamos os olhos pelo texto em busca de informações específicas, como uma data, um nome ou a resposta a uma pergunta.

2 Read the text again. Check the true statements.

1. The MIT Media Lab is unveiling the City Car before the scooter. ☐
2. The City Car is a vehicle that will alleviate congestion. ☐
3. People will use public spaces to fold and stack their vehicles. ☐
4. The MIT group believes the vehicle is not a strategy to mitigate pollution with electric power. ☐

3 Correct the false statements in activity 2.

____

____

____

____

RELATED LINKS

For more information on this Link's topics, please visit:

http://awesome.good.is.s3.amazonaws.com/transparency/web/1107/renewable-energy/flash.html

http://teenstech.com/

4 Check the information which is *not* provided in the text.

1. The kinds of vehicles that will be unveiled. ☐
2. What MIT stands for. ☐
3. The name of the event where the scooter will be presented. ☐

FORUM

How will electric cars help solve the problem of mass transit and pollution?

Do you think they'll be affordable to everyone? Why / Why not?

5 According to William Mitchell, it's correct to infer that...

1. private automobiles are not very sustainable. ☐
2. the Smart Cities group is looking for alternative ways of mobility in the countryside. ☐
3. personal mobility in urban areas is sustainable. ☐

EXPANDING THE *VOCABULARY*

1 Skim the text for words that match the definitions.

1. To make something less difficult or problematic: ____________
2. To show people a new product for the first time: ____________
3. Something planned to happen in the future: ____________
4. Putting things into a pile: ____________
5. The person or thing that is most important in a group: ____________
6. A large wire basket on wheels, used in a supermarket: ____________
7. To make a situation or the effects of something less harmful: ____________

2 Identify the underlined words as *noun*, *adjective*, or *verb*.

1. ...working on two low-cost electric vehicles: ____________
2. ...and help alleviate pollution: ____________
3. A prototype for the team's foldable electric car...: ____________
4. The MIT group sees the vehicles...: ____________; ____________
5. ...in a much more sustainable way: ____________
6. ...and alleviate congestion by letting people rent: ____________

3 Find out what these words have in common. Use some of them to complete the sentences.

rethink	return	rewrite	remake
recycle	react	remarry	recalculate

1. I don't know how to ____________ when he gets angry at me.
2. The teacher wants me to ____________ my composition.
3. Do you ____________ used glass, paper, and plastic?
4. I have to ____________ this book to the library in two days.
5. She will ____________ her dress for her sister's party.
6. Set the GPS to ____________ the route.

Prefixes

O prefixo *re-* significa "novamente; fazer de novo". Forme outras palavras com *fresh*, *model*, *develop*, *assure*, *form*, *cover*, *birth*, *direct*, *group*, *build*, *do*, *arrange*, *type*, *order*, *claim*, *consider*, *take*, *view* e *value*. Escreva frases com essas novas palavras para memorizar o significado delas.

4 Check the best translation for the underlined words in the sentences.

1. They expect to expand limited public space.
   a. esperam ☐ b. têm o aspecto ☐ c. experimentam ☐
2. People will rent and return the vehicles to racks near train stations.
   a. retornarão ☐ b. alugarão ☐ c. devolverão ☐
3. All the essential mechanical systems will be housed in the wheels.
   a. sairão de casa ☐ b. entrarão em casa ☐ c. estarão alojados ☐
4. The research group includes students with backgrounds ranging from architecture to aeronautics.
   a. que recorrem ☐ b. que variam ☐ c. que rangem ☐

5 Check the meaning of the sentences below.

1. The MIT group sees the vehicles as the linchpin in a strategy that aims to mitigate pollution with electric power.
   a. Os veículos são a coisa mais importante numa estratégia que tem o propósito de diminuir a poluição com energia elétrica. ☐
   b. Os veículos são uma coisa importante para atingir a poluição com energia elétrica. ☐
2. A prototype for the team's foldable electric car, called the City Car, is slated to follow next year.
   a. Um protótipo da equipe será lançado no ano seguinte. ☐
   b. Um protótipo chamado City Car será apresentado no próximo ano. ☐

6 Match the meanings with the use of the word "*work*" in the sentences below.

1. a job	☐	Let's go. It's time to begin the day's *work*.
2. a task	☐	Are you looking for *work*?
3. a place	☐	How does this camera *work*?
4. function	☐	I have to talk to you. May I call you at *work*?

7 Check the correct alternative.

1. You and Sally have to *work out* your personal differences.
   a. develop ☐ b. increase ☐ c. solve ☐
2. Let's *work out* a plan to diminish pollution.
   a. result ☐ b. develop ☐ c. influence ☐
3. New financial strategies may not *work out* nowadays.
   a. prove successful ☐ b. influence ☐ c. diminish ☐
4. It *worked out* that everybody left the room at the same time.
   a. solved ☐ b. resulted ☐ c. developed ☐

Work out é *phrasal verb* = um verbo mais uma partícula que modifica o significado desse verbo.

Future Tenses

The group *will* unveil a prototype of its foldable electric scooter at the EICMA Motorcycle Show, in Milan.

Will: expressa previsão de acontecimentos, promessas e decisões tomadas no momento da fala.

*** *will* + verbo no infinitivo sem *to***

Will they unveil a prototype in Milan? / Yes, they *will*. / No, they *won't*.

Where *will* they unveil the prototype? / In Milan.

Be going to: expressa decisões tomadas antes do momento da fala e previsões com base em evidências.

*** verbo *be* + *going to***

The cars *are going to* revolutionize mass transit.

Future Continuous: indica que uma ação estará em progresso em determinado momento no futuro.

*** *will* + *be* + verbo com *-ing***

Tomorrow at ten I *will be driving* to school.

Future Perfect: expressa o momento em que uma ação deverá ter terminado.

*** *will* + *have* + verbo no particípio passado**

By April, I *will have finished* my driving lessons.

1 Match the columns.

1. Louis is going to start a new job.	☐	he'll be traveling to Australia.
2. The children are very tired.	☐	I'm sure he'll enjoy it.
3. Next Monday,	☐	are going to get married next summer.
4. By the end of the month,	☐	They're going to fall asleep quickly.
5. Karen and Mike	☐	she'll have studied the content for Book 1.

2 Read an excerpt from *The Pearl*. Complete the sentences with the future of the verbs from the box.

read	know	make	write	go

[...] Kino looked seriously at his neighbors. "My son ________ to school," he said. The neighbors were silent. Juana's eyes were bright as she watched him. [...] Was this really possible?

But Kino's face shone. "My son ________ and open books, and my son ________ and will know writing.

And my son will make numbers, and these things ________ us free. Because he will know and through him we ________."

Extracted from: *The Pearl*, by John Steinbeck, retold by Gregory McElwain. Penguin Active Reading, 2007, page 16.

Communication Bytes

1 **Sarah is thinking about buying a new car. Listen to her conversation with Matt and answer T for *true* or F for *false*.**

3

S: You know, Matt, I'm thinking about buying a new car.

M: What?

S: Yeah, I need a more modern model. My car is old, and I'm going to lose money if I wait too long to get a new one.

M: You're right. If it gets too old, you won't get good money for it.

S: Will you be working tomorrow afternoon? We could go to the dealership and check out some models.

M: No, I won't. It's my day off, so I can go with you.

S: Perfect!

1. Sarah has evidence she needs a new car. ☐
2. Matt knows what he will be doing in a definite time in the future. ☐
3. Sarah and Matt decided to see the car together. ☐

2 **What kind of plans do people usually make for the future? In your opinion, what are the most important? Rank them from 1 (the most important) to 6 (the least important).**

☐ buy a house

☐ get a college degree

☐ have a well-paid job

☐ build a nice family

☐ travel abroad

☐ buy a car

3 **Now talk to a partner about the plans you have for the future. You can use some of the options in exercise 2.**

LANGUAGE HELP

I think I'll…	I'm going to…
I won't…	In 2032, I'll be …ing …
I'll probably…	By 2020, I will have …

Linked Skills

1 Listen to the weather forecast and choose the correct picture.

4

☐

☐

2 Now write the weather forecast for some Brazilian cities. You can read the transcript for help and use the words/sentences from the box.

sunny	rainy	cloudy	chilly	snowy	windy
The temperature is…		It's… in Recife.		The weather is…	

____

____

____

____

____

Massachusetts Institute of Technology MIT Facts

ORIGINS

The Institute admitted its first students in 1865, four years after the approval of its founding charter. The opening marked the culmination of an extended effort by William Barton Rogers to establish a new kind of independent educational institution relevant to an increasingly industrialized America.

Today MIT is a world-class educational institution. Teaching and research—with relevance to the practical world as a guiding principle—continue to be its primary purpose. MIT is independent, coeducational, and privately endowed. Its five schools and one college encompass numerous academic departments, divisions, and degree-granting programs, as well as interdisciplinary centers, laboratories, and programs whose work cuts across traditional departmental boundaries.

MISSION

The mission of MIT is to advance knowledge and educate students in science, technology, and other areas of scholarship that will best serve the nation and the world in the twenty-first century.

The Institute is committed to generating, disseminating, and preserving knowledge, and to working with others to bring this knowledge to bear on the world's great challenges. MIT is dedicated to providing its students with an education that combines rigorous academic study and the excitement of discovery with the support and intellectual stimulation of a diverse campus community. We seek to develop in each member of the MIT community the ability and passion to work wisely, creatively, and effectively for the betterment of humankind.

Extracted from: http://web.mit.edu/facts/mission.html

Attention!

MIT offers free online courses for students all over the world!

Check them out at http://ocw.mit.edu/index.htm

Think about it!

Why do people choose to take online courses? How can these courses be more efficient than the ones in a regular classroom?

Reading Comprehension

1 **Read the text about MIT again and answer the questions in Portuguese.**

1. What happened in 1865?

____

2. How is MIT known today?

____

3. What is MIT's primary purpose?

____

4. What is MIT's commitment?

____

____

2 **What information can't be found in the text?**

1. Where MIT was meant to be relevant. ☐
2. Roger's occupation. ☐
3. The number of schools in MIT. ☐

3 **Find words in the text that mean**

1. to include a wide range of something (Origins, line 9): ____________
2. real or imaginary lines that mark the edge of something (Origins, line 12): ____________
3. knowledge and learning (Mission, line 2): ____________
4. very severe or strict (Mission, line 7): ____________
5. improvement (Mission, line 11): ____________
6. people in general (Mission, line 11): ____________

4 **Read and answer T for *true* or F for *false*.**

1. *Wisely*, *creatively*, and *effectively* are examples of verbs. ☐
2. *Seek* means "procurar." ☐
3. *Culmination* is when something happens at the end of a period of effort or development. ☐
4. *Discovery* and *stimulation* are not examples of nouns. ☐

Hyperlinks

future + predictions

LINK 2

LOG IN

1 What kind of technological gadgets is part of your daily life?

2 In your opinion, can we believe in predictions? Are they based on facts?

WORD BANK

aware: consciente de algo
blender: liquidificador
chairman: presidente de uma empresa
founder: fundador
gist: assunto
infamous: infame
muffed: mal feito
plywood: madeira compensada
ponder: pensar a respeito, considerar
silly: embaraçoso

NOTES

6 USE IT BETTER: THE WORST TECH PREDICTIONS OF ALL TIME

[...]

By DAVID POGUE

In my Scientific American column this month, I pondered why it's so hard to predict the future of technology. It sometimes seems as though it's not even worth the effort; inevitably you wind up looking like an idiot.

Especially if the gist of your prediction is that something won't happen or isn't possible. You wind up with enough egg on your face to make an omelet.

If you're not convinced, have a look at these whoppers: some of the biggest muffed tech predictions of all time, and spoken by people you'd expect would know better.

"I predict the Internet will soon go spectacularly supernova and in 1996 catastrophically collapse."

Robert Metcalfe, founder of 3Com and inventor of Ethernet, writing in a 1995 *InfoWorld* column

Metcalfe is well aware how silly his prediction came to look. He ate his words — literally. In 1999, addressing the Sixth International WWW Conference, Metcalfe put a copy of his infamous column into a blender, pureed it, and drank it. [...]

"I think there is a world market for maybe five computers."

Thomas Watson, chairman of IBM, 1943

Of course, Watson was referring to room-size mega-machines filled with vacuum tubes. But still. [...]

"This 'telephone' has too many shortcomings to be seriously considered as a means of communication."

Western Union internal memo, 1876

Oops! Western Union sent its last telegram in 2006. [...]

"Television won't be able to hold on to any market it captures after the first six months. People will soon get tired of staring at a plywood box every night."

Darryl Zanuck, 20th Century Fox, 1946

He was right. We've moved on to aluminum and plastic. [...]

Extracted from: http://www.scientificamerican.com/article.cfm?id=pogue-all-time-worst-tech-predictions

UNCOVERING THE *TEXT*

TOPIC

____

GENRE

What kind of text is the one on pages 14 and 15?

- [ ] article
- [ ] biography
- [ ] form
- [ ] instruction manual

Re-reading is a Reading strategy!

Releia o texto quantas vezes forem necessárias para encontrar informações específicas ou para obter uma compreensão global.

RELATED LINKS

For more information on this Link's topics, please visit:

http://www.technewsworld.com/
http://www.scubadiving.com/

FORUM

Since the time of ancient civilizations, humans have tried to make predictions about personal life the afterlife, business, science, and so on. Why is that so? How can that help humanity?

1 Read the sentences and circle what the underlined words refer to.

1. "Television won't be able to hold on to any market <u>it</u> captures after the first six months.
2. Metcalfe put a copy of his infamous column into a blender, pureed <u>it</u>, and drank <u>it</u>.

2 Check the meaning of the underlined words in the context.

1. In 1999, <u>addressing</u> the Sixth International WWW Conference.
   a. falando com [ ] b. endereçado [ ] c. adereço [ ]
2. "People will soon get tired of <u>staring</u> at a plywood box every night."
   a. permanecer [ ] b. olhar fixamente [ ] c. passear [ ]

3 Read the quotes again. Check the probable reasons for those predictions.

1. [3rd prediction] Darryl Zanuck, the movie producer, said that because:
   a. TVs were too ugly at the time. [ ]
   b. he thought people wouldn't like to watch TV for a long time. [ ]
2. [1st prediction] Metcalfe, inventor of Ethernet, said that because:
   a. he didn't know anything about it. [ ]
   b. he had concerns about digital money, speed and capacity. [ ]
3. [2nd prediction] Thomas Watson stated that because:
   a. computers were too big at the time. [ ]
   b. computers were useless at the time. [ ]

4 Think and answer. (Answer in Portuguese or in English.)

1. What is the verb tense generally used for predictions?

   ____

2. Why does the author say the predictions were "spoken by people you'd expect would know better"? Because…

   ____

3. In what types of texts are predictions generally used?

   ____

EXPANDING THE *VOCABULARY*

1 Add *-ing* to the verbs to form adjectives. Then rewrite the phrases.

1. Machines that fly are *flying machines*.
2. A factor that contributes is a ____________________.
3. A movie that involves is an ____________________.
4. A story that interests is an ____________________.
5. A power that stays is a ____________________.

Suffixes

O sufixo *-ing* pode transformar verbos em adjetivos ou substantivos.
Ex.: *Read**ing** is a good pastime.*

2 Form new words using the prefixes and suffixes from the box. Then complete the sentences.

-er	-able	-ion	im-	un-

1. change: *unchange, changeable*
2. found: ____________________
3. possible: ____________________
4. invent: ____________________
5. produce: ____________________
6. questionably: ____________________

1. A: Please, I want to question him about his statements.
   B: Sorry; his statements are ____________ true.
2. A: Who started this industry?
   B: My father was the ____________.
3. A: Can we meet tomorrow?
   B: Tomorrow is ____________. Sorry.

Prefixes and Suffixes

Alguns dos prefixos e sufixos do texto: ***un-*** / ***im-*** / ***in-*** (= não, sem); ***-er*** / ***-or*** (= atividade); ***-able*** / ***-ible*** (= habilidade); ***-ion*** (= condição; ação).

3 Match the false friends to their meanings in Portuguese.

1. prime	( ) função
2. role	( ) prefeito
3. mayor	( ) declarar
4. state (v.)	( ) primeiro

False Friends

Cognatos são palavras com a mesma origem e significado. Quando são diferentes no significado, são chamadas “falsos cognatos” ou “falsos amigos” em português.
Ex.: *ordinary* = comum.

4 **Look at the sentences from the text and choose the sentence where the underlined expression has a different meaning.**

1. There's no chance that the iPhone is going to get any significant market share.
   a. I think there are no chances of rain today. ☐
   b. He had his chance, but he missed it. ☐
2. Darryl Zanuck, a movie producer at 20th Century Fox, said in 1946 that television wouldn't last.
   a. I was late, that's why I'm the last to arrive today. ☐
   b. This new fad won't last much longer. ☐
3. There is no reason anyone would want a computer in their home.
   a. No reason to panic; everything is under control. ☐
   b. Sometimes we have to follow emotion more than reason. ☐
4. It was reported that approximately 80 percent of households in the U.S. had at least one computer.
   a. They want to exercise at least three times a week. ☐
   b. You should, at least, say good-bye. ☐

5 **Choose the best alternative.**

1. A person who is not responsible is...
   a. respectable. ☐ b. restless. ☐ c. irresponsible. ☐
2. When something is good for nothing, it is...
   a. exotic. ☐ b. useless. ☐ c. corrupt. ☐
3. If something is gone, it means...
   a. it has disappeared. ☐ b. it is near. ☐ c. it is in sight. ☐
4. A person who invents something is...
   a. a founder. ☐ b. a creator. ☐ c. an inventor. ☐

DISCOVERING **GRAMMAR**

Indefinites & indefinite compounds

It's a bad Idea to say *something* can't be done.
There is *no* reason anyone would want a computer...

Adjetivos ou pronomes indefinidos são usados para fazer referência a algo de maneira não específica. Alguns deles são:

some (algum[ns], alguma[s]): usado em frases afirmativas ou em interrogativas com expectativa de resposta positiva. I bought *some* flowers. / Would you like *some* tea?

any (algum[ns], nenhum[a], alguma[s]): usado em frases interrogativas e negativas; frases com *if*; com o significado de "qualquer". Do you have *any* experience? / I don't have *any* idea. / If you have *any* problems, just ask me. / Choose *any* book you want.

no, none (nenhum[a]): usado para dar sentido negativo à frase. You have *no* idea. (adj.) / I have *none*. (pron.)

Os **compounds** (compostos) de **some**, **any** e **no** seguem as mesmas regras de uso desses adjetivos e pronomes indefinidos.

- ***somebody/someone, anybody/anyone, nobody/no one (pessoas)*** I need *somebody* to love. / Is there *anyone* home? / There's *nobody* home.
- ***something, anything, nothing (coisas)*** I can do *something* to help you. / Is there *anything* I can do? / I can do *nothing* to help you.
- ***somewhere, anywhere, nowhere (lugares)*** The book is *somewhere* under the bed. / I can't find it *anywhere*. / I can find it *nowhere*.

1 Underline the correct alternatives.

1. They have *no / none* money. They are broke.
2. I haven't seen *no / any* ghosts.
3. Cookies? There are *no / none*.
4. Is there *any / no* milk in the fridge?

2 Read the excerpt from *The Phantom of the Opera*. Fill in the blanks with an indefinite compound.

They could hear (1) somebody outside the door. Sorelli went up to it and in a shaky voice asked, "Who's there?" But (2) ___________ answered. Feeling all eyes on her, she asked loudly, "Is (3) ___________ behind the door?"

Sorelli turned the key and opened the door. She bravely looked into the passage. It was empty. She closed the door.

"No," she said, "there is (4) ___________ there."

Source: The Phantom of the Opera, by Gaston Leroux, retold by Coleen Degnan-Veness. Penguin Readers, 2008, page 2.

Predictions

1 **Some sites publish people's predictions about the future. Read the predictions and check the ones you agree with.**

Prediction	Duration	Predictor
By 2020, bioterror or bioerror will lead to one million casualties in a single event. ☐	2002-2020	Martin Rees
By 2050, we will receive intelligent signals from outside our solar system. ☐	2002-2050	Paul Hawken
By 2030, all surgical anesthesia will be administered and monitored by computers, with no need for professional medical supervision beyond the surgeon. ☐	2002-2030	Jason I. Altman
By 2100, racism will no longer be a significant phenomenon in most countries of the world. ☐	2003-2100	Bill Moore
One hundred years from now, a person will live anywhere on Earth if they agree to obey local laws. ☐	2003-2103	Kevin Kelly

Source: www.longbets.org/predictions

2 **Write two predictions for the future. Determine the year they will happen. The words below may help.**

By (year)… there will be will be over peace war countries children poverty forests population of humans on Earth Latin America tallest building families marriage politicians Mars global warming space travel

____

____

____

____

____

WORD BANK

lead: levar
beyond: além de
no longer: não mais
single: único

Review

1 **Check the correct alternative.**

1. Marina ________________ a new car this weekend.
   a. will to buy ☐
   b. will buys ☐
   c. is going buy ☐
   d. going to buy ☐
   e. is going to buy ☐
2. "He is likely to move to another city" means...
   a. he will not move to another city. ☐
   b. he prefers to move to another city. ☐
   c. he enjoys moving to different cities. ☐
   d. he will probably move to another city. ☐
   e. he frequently moves to other cities. ☐
3. "Jill will start a new course next month" in the negative form is...
   a. Jill don't will start a new course next month. ☐
   b. Jill doesn't will start a new course next month. ☐
   c. Jill don't will start a new course next month. ☐
   d. Jill won't start a new course next month. ☐
   e. Jill not start a new course next month. ☐
4. She didn't have ________________ mistakes in her last exercise.
   a. some ☐
   b. no ☐
   c. nothing ☐
   d. any ☐
   e. no one ☐
5. Take it. There is ________________ better for your headache than this pill.
   a. none ☐
   b. nothing ☐
   c. anybody ☐
   d. nobody ☐
   e. any ☐
6. She hates everybody! She loves ________________.
   a. nobody ☐
   b. someone ☐
   c. somebody ☐
   d. anyone ☐
   e. something ☐
7. They'll call me if ________________ goes wrong.
   a. nowhere ☐
   b. anything ☐
   c. somebody ☐
   d. nobody ☐
   e. any ☐

Self-Contained Underwater Breathing Apparatus, or Scuba Diving

Scuba Destinations: Brazil

Scuba is an acronym for Self-Contained Underwater Breathing Apparatus.

In 1943, Émile Gagnan and Jacques Cousteau created the scuba diving kit we know today (diving suit and breathing system).

[…] Good scuba diving can be found at Arraial do Cabo; the Abrolhos Archipelago; Boipeba; Porto Belo in Santa Catarina; and Joao Pessoa, in Paraiba.

WORD BANK

diver: mergulhador
pinnacle: pináculo, torre
reef: recife
scuba diving: mergulho (com o equipamento apropriado)
wreck: naufrágio

Good diving areas are:

Arraial do Cabo – […] this city is well known among Brazilian scuba divers and anybody who loves to be around the sea. White sand beaches and great visibility. With 47 shipwrecks in the region to explore, there are plenty of options. […]

Fernando de Noronha – […] a fabulous archipelago in the Northeast and a protected marine park. The best time of the year for diving is from July to December for beginners, all year round for advanced divers. […] Prolific marine life is found – pelagics such as tuna, jack, albacore, barracuda, and others. […]

The Abrolhos Archipelago – […] a Marine National Park located 45 miles off the mid-eastern coast of Brazil, [it] consists of five volcanic islands and is home to the greatest chains of coral reefs in the South Atlantic. […] There is no other place on Earth where you can see the type of coral reef pinnacle prevalent in Abrolhos waters.

Extracted from: www.scubadviser.com/destinations_1.aspx?id=1:35219&doc=0:37330

2 **Listen and read the text. Write down something you learned about scuba diving in Portuguese or English.**

____

____

3 **Scan the text to answer the questions below.**

1. How many shipwrecks can divers find in Arraial do Cabo?

____

2. Where can we find a special type of coral reef?

____

3. Where is Fernando de Noronha?

____

4. What can we find in Boipeba?

____

5. What does *scuba* stand for?

____

4 **Check the sentence that is correct according to the text.**

1. Five volcanic islands form Abrolhos. ☐
2. Scuba diving is practiced only in Brazil. ☐
3. Boipeba is not a good diving area. ☐
4. There is no marine life in Fernando de Noronha. ☐

5 **Check T for *true* or F for *false*.**

1. There are some good diving areas in Brazil. ☐
2. There aren't any good diving areas in Brazil. ☐
3. Brazilian scuba divers know Arraial do Cabo. ☐
4. Beginners can dive all year round in Fernando de Noronha. ☐

6 **What can we infer from the underlined part of the sentence below?**

"In 1943, Émile Gagnan and Jacques Cousteau created <u>the scuba diving kit we know today</u>."

1. Gagnan and Cousteau were the first who tried to create an apparatus for diving. ☐
2. Other types of diving apparatus existed. ☐
3. Only Cousteau and Gagnan wanted to breath underwater. ☐

So far, so good?

Use the code and discover the names of the diving apparatus below.

A	B	C	D	E	F	G	H	I	J	K	L	M
▲	◘	▼	☻	◊	○	●	☺	◙	◀	☼	Σ	▶
N	**O**	**P**	**Q**	**R**	**S**	**T**	**U**	**V**	**W**	**X**	**Y**	**Z**
Δ	♠	€	♥	□	♪	♫	♦	#	♣	£	π	Ω

Scuba Diving Timeline			
year	**invention**		
500 B.C.	Men use a hollow reed as →	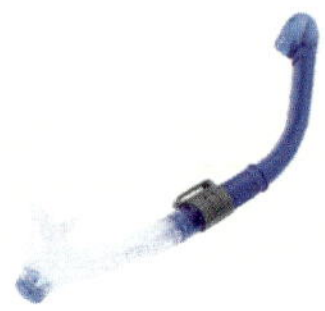	♪ Δ ♠ □ ☼ ◊ Σ ___ ___ ___ ___ ___ ___ ___
332 B.C.	People invent the 1st →		☻ ◙ # ◙ Δ ● ◘ ◊ Σ Σ ___ ___ ___ ___ ___ ___ ___ ___ ___ ___
1300 A.D.	Persians invent →		◊ π ◊ ● ♠ ● ● Σ ◊ ♪ ___ ___ ___ ___ ___ ___ ___ ___ ___ ___
1715	Lethbridge invents one-man →		☻ ◙ # ◙ Δ ● ◊ Δ ● ◙ Δ ◊ ___ ___ ___ ___ ___ ___ ___ ___ ___ ___ ___ ___
1829	John and Charles Deane invent the →		☻ ◙ # ◙ Δ ● ☺ ◊ Σ ▶ ◊ ♫ ___ ___ ___ ___ ___ ___ ___ ___ ___ ___ ___ ___

Extracted from: http://aquaviews.net/scuba-guides/evolution-modern-scuba-gear-ages/

Now that I've finished links 1 and 2, I can…

…express future plans and events.	☐ Yes!	☐ I still need to study more!
…talk about indefinite quantities.	☐ Yes!	☐ I still need to study more!
…create adjectives and nouns using prefixes and suffixes.	☐ Yes!	☐ I still need to study more!

Hyperlinks

differences + culture

LINK 3

LOG IN

1 Take a look at these two pages—images, titles, text—and answer: What is the text about?

2 Do we usually respect other people's cultures and religions?

WORD BANK

advice: conselho
belong: pertencer
keep: manter
share: compartilhar
step: passo
truly: verdadeiramente
understanding: compreensão
value: valor
who else: quem mais
whose: cujo(a)
worth: valor

NOTES

A Letter from the Secretary General

8

What Can You Do?

More and more, young people are asking me this encouraging question: What can I do to make things better? My advice is start by learning and looking around you. Get to know people whose lives are different from yours. Find out what you have in common with them. Build **bridges** of understanding with them. It is only by doing so that we can truly appreciate the worth of others. [...]

Computers and modems help us talk and listen to each other across oceans. But that would not do us much good if we did not already have a lot in common. Every society needs shared values: For our global society, that is respect for our equal human rights. We may have different **religions**, different languages, different coloured skins—but we all belong to one human race. We are all part of the same human family—and when one part of that family does well, we all do better. So we want to help others to have the same opportunities we have.

Once you have created a bridge with others, keep it open by talking to each other and, above all, by listening. This is what I try to do [...] because I know that once I have built up trust with someone, we can work to change things together. So can you. When you see something that is wrong, no matter how big the problem is, ask yourself: Who else would like to change this? How can we work together? Take action with others who share your conviction. Have the courage to believe you can make a difference. As with everything in life, small steps count. If something has not been done before, it does not mean it can't be done; it only means you could be the first to do it.

Kofi Annan

Secretary General (1997-2006)
United Nations

Extracted from: Remarks made at the Festival Mondial des Enfants in Basel, Switzerland, 24 June 2000

UNCOVERING THE *TEXT*

TOPIC

____

GENRE

What kind of the text is the one on page 27?

- [ ] article
- [ ] blog
- [ ] interview
- [ ] letter

Predicting is a reading strategy!

Examinar os elementos que compõem um texto antes de lê-lo pode nos ajudar a fazer previsões sobre as informações e o conteúdo geral que vamos encontrar.

RELATED LINKS

For more information on this Link's topics, please visit:

http://www.unitedplanet.org/
http://www.partnershipfor-globaljustice.com/

FORUM

How can we show respect for people and things at school or in our community?

What do you think is wrong around you? Can you find people who agree with you and think of an action plan?

1 Take a look at pages 26 and 27. Check the elements that help us make predictions about the text.

1. vocabulary ☐
2. images ☐
3. titles ☐
4. layout ☐

2 Read the first lines of the text on page 27. Who does Kofi Annan address?

1. politicians ☐ 2. young people ☐ 3. women ☐

3 Search the text and check what the underlined words refer to.

1. My advice is, start by learning and looking around you. (1st paragraph)
   a. the secretary general ☐ b. young people ☐
2. Get to know people whose lives are different from yours. (1st paragraph)
   a. the people's lives ☐ b. your life ☐
3. We may have different religions, different coloured skins. (2nd paragraph)
   a. the American people ☐ b. people in general ☐

4 Check the information which is not provided in the text.

1. Young people don't care about helping the world. ☐
2. An increasing number of young people want to help make things better. ☐
3. We should help people build houses and bridges. ☐
4. According to Mr. Annan, small steps can make a difference. ☐
5. We have to do something big to make a difference. ☐

5 Answer the questions to express your opinion.

1. Do you agree with Mr. Annan's ideas? Can small steps make a difference?

   ____

2. Is it easy to make bridges of understanding? Why?

   ____

EXPANDING THE *VOCABULARY*

1 Complete the sentences with the verbs from the box.

take	do	~~make~~	build

1. We don't know how we can ___make___ things better.
2. If different countries ______ bridges of understanding, the world will be a better place.
3. I hope we ______ really well on the test tomorrow.
4. You can't just sit and wait! You must ______ action and solve this problem.

Collocations

São palavras geralmente usadas em conjunto:

do: homework, business, your best, a favor

make: the bed, a mistake, an appointment

2 Read the sentence: "More and more, young people are asking me this encouraging question." The word *encouraging* means "something that gives courage." Substitute the italicized words to rewrite the sentences. Use *en-* / *em-* verbs.

1. I'm going to make it *larger*. ___I'm going to enlarge it___.
2. We are going to give him *courage*. ______.
3. Adjectives make a text *rich*. ______.
4. The new job can give him *power*. ______.

Prefixes

Os prefixos ***en-*** / ***em-*** indicam **pôr dentro**; **dentro**; **fornecer**.

Ex.: ***en****joy*.

Forme outras palavras com: *force, capsulate, cage, code.*

3 Complete the sentences with the words from the box.

advise (v.)	advice (n.)	human (n.)	humane (adj.)

1. The ___Humane___ Society of the United States (HSUS) is the nation's largest animal protection organization.
2. Follow my ______ and don't talk to her now.
3. They always ______ us to buckle our seatbelts.
4. He is so horrible that I don't think he is ______.

Confusing Words

Algumas palavras são facilmente confundidas, portanto preste atenção aos detalhes:

apart (adv.) = separado:

How far apart are the two cities?

a part (n.) = uma parte de:

A part of my heart left when he did.

4 Explain, in Portuguese, the underlined expression.

Build <u>bridges of understanding</u> with them.

______

______

______

______

5 **Match the words with the definitions.**

1. respectfully
2. respectable
3. respectful
4. respect

☐ to feel or show deferential regard for
☐ politely and with respect
☐ deserving respect
☐ showing respect

6 **Check the general idea of the sentences below.**

	Comparison	Cause	Manner
1. As with everything in life, small steps count.	✓		
2. What can you do to make things better? Start by looking around you.			
3. It is only by doing so that we can appreciate the worth of others.			
4. Every society needs shared values because we all belong to one human race.			

7 **Complete the sentences with words from the box. Then choose pictures that illustrate them.**

around from with for

1. What do you have in common ____________ your classmates?
2. Look ____________ you and ask yourself how you can help make things better.
3. Do you respect people whose lives are different ____________ yours?
4. One of our values should be respect ____________ equal human rights.

a.  ☐

c.  ☐

b.  ☐

d.  ☐

DISCOVERING *GRAMMAR*

Modal Verbs

We *may* have different religions.
We *can* work to change things together.

Os verbos modais auxiliam outros verbos a expressar conceitos.

can: expressa habilidade e permissão no presente. You *can* go to your friend's house. / I *can't* drive because I'm not eighteen.

could: expressa habilidade e permissão no passado. They *could* study together last weekend. / She *could* cook when she was fourteen.

may: indica possibilidade. I *may* travel this weekend.

might: indica possibilidade, mas em intensidade menor que ***may.***
He *might* visit them tomorrow, but he'll probably go next week.

must: indica uma obrigação intrínseca ao sujeito falante e uma proibição quando na negativa.
We *must* finish our homework before midnight. / You *mustn't* enter this area.

ought to: indica uma sugestão. It may rain; you *ought to* take an umbrella.

should: indica um conselho. You *should* take some cough syrup for that cough of yours.

Os verbos modais obedecem a uma mesma regra estrutural:

Affirmative: sujeito + verbo modal + verbo no infinitivo sem *to* + complemento
He *can* swim.

Negative: sujeito + verbo modal + not + verbo no infinitivo sem *to* + complemento
He *can't* swim.

Interrogative: verbo modal + sujeito + verbo no infinitivo sem *to* + complemento
Can he swim?

1 Check the meaning of the modal verbs in the sentences.

1. They ought to go straight back home.
   a. habilidade ☐ b. sugestão ☐ c. proibição ☐
2. I must leave now.
   a. habilidade ☐ b. obrigação ☐ c. opinião ☐
3. You should stay in bed for a couple of days.
   a. conselho ☐ b. dedução ☐ c. habilidade ☐
4. He may go to the beach if he doesn't have to work.
   a. possibilidade ☐ b. conselho ☐ c. permissão ☐

Communication Bytes

1 Ricky is concerned about some recent problems occurring in his neighborhood. He wrote an e-mail to the people who live there. Read and listen to it. 9

Hi, everyone!

I don't know if you have already seen, although I believe it's very hard not to, but the number of people living on the streets in our neighborhood is increasing. We usually tend to ignore them and just live our lives as if they didn't exist, but most of the people I had the chance to talk to personally feel less safe walking around because of them. I also heard some people talking about calling the police and things like that. So, I decided to look for other options we might have besides the police. I learned there is a center called CENTRO POP, specially made for people who live on the streets. I think we should try to contact them and see if they can send some people here to help them. What do you think?

I don't have many contacts from our area, so can you please forward this message to people you know that live around here?

I hope we can do something about this as fast as possible.

Sincerely,

Ricky

2 **Answer T for *true* or F for *false*.**

1. Ricky lives on the street. ☐
2. Ricky wants to call the police to solve the situation. ☐
3. Ricky did research on what to do about this situation. ☐
4. Ricky has lots of contacts from his neighborhood. ☐

3 **Think about a problem you face in your school or your school's neighborhood and write an e-mail to your friends in the classroom expressing your concern about this. Offer them a possible solution. You can use the words and expressions below to help you.**

I want to express my concern about…
I'm really worried about…
You must have noticed that…
We should all get together and…

____
____
____
____
____

Linked Skills

1 Listen to some proverbs and match the parts to make the complete sentences. 10

1.	Love is the art	☐	they will respect you.
2.	Love is incompatible	☐	of making exceptions.
3.	If you respect others,	☐	should be treated with respect.
4.	Good actions are nourishment for youths,	☐	blind; friendship closes its eyes.
5.	Love is	☐	with fear.
6.	The old	☐	much more than words.

2 What's your opinion about proverbs 1 and 4? Justify your answers.

____

____

____

____

____

Useful expressions

I strongly agree / disagree with…; In my opinion…; I think…; I agree / disagree with… because…

3 Talk to a classmate about the proverb you liked most. Explain why. Use the language box below to help you.

I liked the proverb, "…" because …
We can't live without…
We have to…
The world today…
Nowadays, we have to think about…

UNITED NATIONS COMPETENCIES FOR THE FUTURE

What are the UN core values and competencies?

11

[...]

These are some of the characteristics that you will find in our staff.

We want people with integrity. People who are fair, impartial, honest and truthful. We want dynamic and adaptable persons who are not afraid to think creatively, to be proactive, flexible and responsive.

If you think you embody these values, then this is the place for you and your career.

Extracted from: https://careers.un.org/lbw/home.aspx?viewtype=WWLF

Extracted from: https://careers.un.org/lbw/attachments/competencies_booklet_en.pdf

Core Values
- ✔ Integrity
- ✔ Professionalism
- ✔ Respect for Diversity

Core Competencies
- ✔ Communication
- ✔ Teamwork
- ✔ Planning & Organizing
- ✔ Accountability
- ✔ Creativity
- ✔ Client Orientation
- ✔ Commitment to Continuous Learning
- ✔ Technological Awareness

Managerial Competencies
- ✔ Leadership
- ✔ Vision
- ✔ Empowering Others
- ✔ Building Trust
- ✔ Managing Performance
- ✔ Judgement/Decision-making

Attention!

If you want more information on the competencies and job vacancies at the UN, access https://careers.un.org/lbw/Home.aspx.

Reading Comprehension

1 Skim the text and answer.

1. O texto…
   a. explica o trabalho desenvolvido pela ONU. ☐
   b. lista as características da ONU. ☐
   c. lista as competências e valores requeridos para trabalhar na ONU. ☐
   d. explica por que determinadas competências são importantes. ☐
   e. lista características comuns a pessoas de sucesso. ☐

2 Scan the text and check what these words refer to.

1. leadership, empowering others, and judgement
   a. managerial competencies ☐
   b. core values ☐
2. teamwork and creativity
   a. core values ☐
   b. core competencies ☐

3 Scan the text and find out words with the suffixes below.

-ity	-ing

4 What competencies do you feel you already have and which ones do you need to develop? How can you develop these competencies?

____

____

____

____

____

Hyperlinks

differences + culture

LINK 4

LOG IN

1 Are laws the same in every country around the world?

2 Is it important to know local laws before traveling to other countries?

WORD BANK

blame: culpar
chomp: mascar
coin: moeda (de metal)
damage: danificar
disease: doença
display: demonstração
feature: destacar
fine: multa
frown: franzir as sobrancelhas
inhaler: inalador
pigeon: pombo
underwear: roupa de baixo

NOTES

12

International Laws
You'd Never Know Were Real

You might want to remember these [...] surprising and strange laws next time you're traveling to avoid embarrassment, fines, or worse!

By JACKIE MIDDLETON

Japan

In Japan, over-the-counter allergy/sinus medications that contain the ingredient pseudoephedrine such as Vicks inhalers and Sudafed are banned under Japan's strict anti-stimulant drug laws. [...]

Italy

Be careful where you consume a relaxing lunch or refreshing beverage in Italy. It's an offense in Florence to eat or drink while sitting on church steps or within a church courtyard. [...]

San Francisco

It's illegal to feed pigeons on the streets of San Francisco. The city famous for the Golden Gate Bridge blames the ubiquitous birds for spreading disease and damaging property. [...]

Maldives

In the Maldives, public observance of any religion other than Islam is prohibited, and it's an offense to import Bibles into the country. [...]

Kazakhstan

In Kazakhstan, [...] [p]hotography in and around airports is illegal, and taking pictures of military and official buildings is frowned upon as well.

The United Arab Emirates

Public displays of affection – kissing, hugging, holding hands – should be avoided while traveling in the United Arab Emirates. [...]
[...] Clothes should cover the tops of the arms and legs, and underwear should not be visible. [...]

Singapore

Smoking laws are more severe in Singapore than they are in North America. Lighting up in public [...] will earn a stiff fine in this Asian country. [...]
It's illegal to chomp gum while riding on Singapore's Mass Rapid Transit (MRT) system, and like smoking, this offense is punishable with a fine.

France

Concealing the face in public places in France is illegal. This includes e.g. balaclavas,* full veils, or any other garment or mask [...].

* Balaclava = gorro de lã que cobre totalmente a cabeça, deixando só os olhos à mostra.

Barcelona

Don't wander away from the Barcelona seafront dressed in just your bikini or swim trunks. In this Spanish city, it's against the law to wear swimming attire on public streets. [...]

Canada

[...] According to Canada's Currency Act, stores can legally refuse excessive amounts of coins. [...]

Extracted from: www.rd.com/slideshows/13-funny-international-laws-youd-never-know-were-real/
www.gov.uk/foreign-travel-advice

UNCOVERING THE TEXT

TOPIC

____

GENRE

What kind of text is on pages 38 and 39?

- [ ] a constitutional code
- [ ] diary notes
- [ ] a report
- [ ] travel information

1 Scan the text for the following information.

1. The place where photography in airports is illegal: ____________
2. The place where it is illegal to feed pigeons: ____________
3. The place where it is against the law to show affection publicly: ____________
5. The place where you can't wear a swimming suit on the streets: ____________

Scanning is a reading strategy!

Passar os olhos pelo texto é uma estratégia útil quando se busca por informações específicas: locais, datas, nomes etc.

2 What are the main characteristics of a travel information text? Check the correct answers.

1. the use of formal language [ ]
2. the use of technical words [ ]
3. verbs in the present or future tenses [ ]
4. informal, direct language [ ]
5. the use of adjectives [ ]

3 Travel information is usually found

1. in blogs, magazines, and travel agencies websites [ ]
2. in books, on social networks (Facebook, Twitter, LinkedIn), and on TV [ ]

RELATED LINKS

For more information on this Link's topics, please visit:

http://itthing.com/100-weird-laws-from-around-the-world
http://www.letterwritingguide.com/

4 Check the correct answer.

1. "An over-the-counter medication" is
   a. medication kept out of sight. [ ]
   b. medication you don't need a medical prescription to buy. [ ]
2. "Public observance of any religion other than Islam is prohibited" means
   a. Islam is not prohibited. [ ]
   b. any religion can be practiced. [ ]
3. "Taking pictures of official buildings is frowned upon" means
   a. local people show that they like it. [ ]
   b. local people show that they dislike it. [ ]

FORUM

Why do people criticize other people's cultures?

EXPANDING THE *VOCABULARY*

1 Form antonyms by adding *-less* to the nouns. Then write the translations for the antonyms.

noun	adjective	antonym	translation
hope	hopeful	hopeless	*desesperançado*
pain	painful		
help	helpful		
fear	fearful		
color	colorful		
faith	faithful		
fruit	fruitful		

Suffixes

O sufixo *-ful* forma adjetivos e significa "cheio de" ou "que tem".

Ex.: *power**ful*** (poderoso), *use**ful*** (útil), *beauti**ful*** (belo).

O sufixo *-less* forma adjetivos e significa "falta de".
Ex.: *power**less*** (fraco), *use**less*** (inútil), *top**less*** (sem a parte de cima).

2 Complete the sentences by adding *-ful* or *-less* to the nouns.

1. Be *careful* (care)! That is a very expensive vase.
2. He is so ____________ (care)! He broke my mother's favorite vase!
3. She is the most ____________ (beauty) girl I know.
4. We have started a campaign to help the ____________ (home) people in town.

3 Circle the words the underlined pronouns refer to.

1. In Japan, over-the-counter allergy medications <u>that</u> contain the ingredient pseudoephedrine are banned.
2. In the UAE, people <u>who</u> show affection on the streets may be fined.
3. France, <u>which</u> is a European country, doesn't allow people to wear veils.

4 Find a word or expression in the text that means...

1. humiliation, shame: ____________.
2. liquid refreshment: ____________.
3. violation, hard feelings: ____________.
4. forbid, ban, restrict: ____________.
5. culpable: ____________.

5 Check the best translation for the underlined words.

1. Don't wander away from the Barcelona seafront dressed in just your bikini or swim trunks.
   a. trabalhar ☐ b. mergulhar ☐ c. perambular ☐
2. In Canada, stores can legally refuse excessive amounts of coins.
   a. quantidades ☐ b. montes ☐ c. montante ☐
3. Public observance of any religion other than Islam is prohibited.
   a. do que ☐ b. outra que não ☐ c. outra ☐
4. Lighting up in public will earn a stiff fine in this Asian country.
   a. acender (cigarro) / severa ☐
   b. observar raios / flexível ☐
   c. iluminar / belo ☐

6 In the sentence "taking pictures of military and official buildings is frowned upon as well," we have the phrasal verb *frowned upon*, which means "to disapprove of something." Look at some other phrasal verbs using *upon* and choose the correct translation.

Em todos os casos nesse exercício, o *phrasal verb* pode ser construído com ***on*** em vez de *upon*. Ex.: *You can't rely just on one player for the whole game.*

1. The kids *looked upon* him as a hero.
   a. considerar ☐
   b. procurar ☐
2. You can't *rely* just *upon* one player for the whole game.
   a. confiar ☐
   b. depender ☐
3. Her parents *prevailed upon* her to clean the house.
   a. prevalecer ☐
   b. persuadir ☐
4. When I first *hit upon* my idea for the project, I didn't even think it would really work out.
   a. ter uma ideia inesperadamente, sem intenção ☐
   b. bater ☐

DISCOVERING *GRAMMAR*

Relative pronouns

Be careful *where* you consume a relaxing lunch.
Medications *that* contain pseudoephedrine are banned.

Os pronomes relativos são usados para ligar duas orações e podem formar dois tipos de relação nas frases:

Defining Relative Clauses	Non-defining Relative Clauses
Nesse tipo de relação, como o nome indica, a oração iniciada pelo *relative pronoun* adiciona uma informação que define o antecedente. Sem essa informação, a frase não teria o mesmo sentido. I know a **woman** → *who* works at the hospital. I lost the **CD** → *that* you lent me. He's the **man** → *whose* wife is a writer.	Nesses casos, a oração iniciada pelo *relative pronoun* não define o antecedente, apenas acrescenta mais informações sobre ele. Caso ela não estivesse lá, ainda saberíamos exatamente quem é o antecedente. Tais orações: • vêm entre ou após virgula(s): Jeff, who is very young, is a doctor. • não omitem o pronome: My new bike, which I bought last week, is fantastic. • não usam **that**: Regis, who you know very well, is coming over later.

O uso dos pronomes varia de acordo com seu antecedente e da função que têm na frase. Observe a tabela:

Antecedente	Pronoun
pessoas	sujeito: *who, that* objeto: *who(m), that*, pronome oculto posse: *whose*
coisas, animais	sujeito: *which, that* objeto: *which, that*, pronome oculto posse: *whose*
lugares	sujeito/objeto: *where, in which*

1 Underline the correct pronouns to complete the sentences.

1. I like games *which* / *who* have a lot of action.
2. That is the girl *who* / *whose* brother broke both legs.
3. He told us about the place *whom* / *where* he was born.
4. I can't find the pen *whose* / *that* you lent me yesterday.
5. That's the hospital *that* / *where* I was born.
6. Do you know the guy *whose* / *who* brought the kayak?
7. I did not mention the person to *who* / *whom* I gave the watch.

Quando o pronome relativo é objeto da oração, podemos usar *whom* em vez de *who*. Ex.: *The girl* ***whom*** *I met lives far from here.*

Asking for Advice

1 **Jenny is traveling and sent an e-mail to her mother. Read the e-mail and answer the questions.** (13)

To: smithmeggy@supermail.com
From: jenny.smith@mymail.com
Attachments Emoticons Tools

Hey mom,

This is my third week in Trinidad and Tobago and I love it. Last week, in Trinidad, I visited Maracas Beach, and it's beautiful! Yesterday, in Tobago, I explored the capital, Scarborough, and it was very nice. But then I ran into some problems. Do you remember I have a camouflage pattern skirt? Just like the camouflage pattern they use in the army, right? I was wearing it, but guess what: it is illegal! Yes, it's true! It's illegal to wear camouflage patterns here in Trinidad and Tobago, and I didn't know that. So, I managed to go back to the hotel and changed clothes. Can you believe that? I tried to contact you over telephone, but I couldn't. I need some help because I don't know what to do: should I stay here for a few more days or just go home? If I stay, I'll need extra money, because I had to pay a fine because of the skirt. Answer as soon as possible, OK?

I really miss you and dad!

See you soon.

Love,

Jenny

1. What is Jenny's problem?

____

2. Why did she receive a fine?

____

2 **Write an e-mail stating a problem you had, or invent one, based on the difference of cultural customs. Use the text "International Laws You'd Never Know Were Real" to help you think of a situation, and ask for some advice on how to solve your problem.**

Review

1 **Choose the correct alternatives to complete the sentences.**

1. I know the girl ______________ wrote you this letter.
   a. which ☐ b. whose ☐ c. when ☐ d. who ☐ e. where ☐
2. We're going to visit a small town ______________ the people speak a local dialect.
   a. whose ☐ b. who ☐ c. whom ☐ d. that ☐ e. in which ☐
3. Are you the guest ______________ is staying at the Plaza Hotel?
   a. which ☐ b. that ☐ c. pronome oculto ☐ d. whose ☐ e. whom ☐

2 **Join the sentences using relative pronouns.**

1. The man was sitting next to me. He was talking to himself.

   ____

2. Those are the students. They won first prize.

   ____

3. He brought me the books. I needed them.

   ____

4. My friend got a new puppy. The puppy's name is Jewel.

   ____

3 **Write one sentence about what you mustn't do in the following situations or places.**

1. Funeral

   ____

2. Job interview

   ____

3. Classroom

   ____

4. Cinema

   ____

5. On the bus

   ____

Review

4 **Read the descriptions and number the corresponding pictures. Then check if the relative clause is defining or non-defining. When there is more than one relative clause, use the underlined one as reference.**

1. The Palace of Westminster, whose name derives from Westminster Abbey, is in London.
   a. defining ☐ b. non-defining ☐
2. Ernest Hemingway (1899 - 1961) was an American author who wrote *The Old Man and the Sea*.
   a. defining ☐ b. non-defining ☐
3. Many articles have featured the story of Oliver, who was a common chimpanzee that displayed some human-like characteristics.
   a. defining ☐ b. non-defining ☐
4. Charlize Theron, who is a South African actress and fashion model, started her acting career in the United States and rose to fame in the late 1990s.
   a. defining ☐ b. non-defining ☐
5. The Sydney Opera House, which is a performing arts center, is in Sydney, Australia.
   a. defining ☐ b. non-defining ☐
6. Betsy is a black and white longhaired border collie that is regarded as one of the smartest animals in history. She can decipher a word after hearing it only twice.
   a. defining ☐ b. non-defining ☐

5 Complete the miniconversations using modal verbs.

1. **A:** Hi, ______________ you help me, please?

   B: Sure, what ______________ I do for you?

   A: I'm late. What is the best way to get to Collins Avenue?

   B: Well, just go straight ahead. I think you ______________ call someone telling you will be late, for it's still a long way to go.

2. **A:** OK, you can go to your friend's house, but remember: you ______________ do all the homework—and don't stay up too late, OK? Tomorrow morning, you ______________ go to the dentist. Don't forget your obligations!

   B: Thanks, Mom. Hey, ______________ you take me to the dentist? I really don't want to go by bus.

   A: No problem.

3. **A:** What a bad cold you have there! You ______________ see a doctor about it.

   B: I know. I have an appointment at three.

4. **A:** I don't know what to do. ______________ I stay here or ______________ I go with you?

   B: Well. You ______________ complete your obligations, and I ______________ go right now. I don't have any other option. So, I think you ______________ stay.

6 What do you think the following people should do?

1. I don't know where I left my glasses.

   ____

2. We don't know where we are.

   ____

3. My dog is sick.

   ____

4. I don't know what to do when I finish high school.

   ____

5. I always wake up late.

   ____

So far, SO GOOD?

1 **Match the pictures to the sentences.**

It might rain today.

I could ride a bike when I was little.

You should eat something.

I can play the drums.

We must brush our teeth after meals.

They shouldn't drive so fast. It's dangerous, and they might hurt other people.

You must stop!

You must dress properly for a job interview.

Now that I've finished links 3 and 4, I can…

…use modal verbs.	☐ Yes!	☐ I still need to study more!
…express myself about people, things, and places in more complex sentences.	☐ Yes!	☐ I still need to study more!
…use suffixes *en-*, *-ful* and *-less*.	☐ Yes!	☐ I still need to study more!

Hyperlinks

inventions + imagination

LINK 5

LOG IN

1 What do you know about the Middle Ages?

2 What's the best invention in the world, in your opinion?

WORD BANK

distaff: fuso de fiar
frames: armação de óculos
lawsuit: ação judicial, processo
loom: tear
portrait: quadro, retrato
presses: prensas
spinning wheel: roca, roda de fiar
steam: vapor
yarn: fio de costura

NOTES

14 Inventions of the Middle Ages

The millennium between the collapse of the Western Roman Empire in the 5th century AD and the beginning of the colonial expansion of Western Europe in the late fifteenth century has been known traditionally as the Middle Ages, and the first half of this period consists of the five centuries of the Dark Ages. We now know that this period was not as socially stagnant as this title suggests. [...]

Extracted from: Encyclopaedia Britannica, 15th edition, 1974 – Macropaedia, volume XVIII, page 32.

Spinning wheel

[...] The spinning wheel was probably invented in India, though its origins are obscure. It reached Europe via the Near East in the Middle Ages. It replaced the earlier method of hand spinning, in which the individual fibers were drawn out of a mass of wool held on a stick, or distaff, twisted together to form a continuous strand, and wound on a second stick, or spindle. [...] The improvement of the loom in 18th-century Britain created a yarn shortage and a demand for mechanical spinning; the result was a series of inventions that converted the spinning wheel into a powered, mechanized component of the industrial revolution.

Extracted from: Encyclopaedia Britannica, 15th edition, 1974 – Micropaedia, volume IX, pages 424-25.

Eyeglasses

[...] Magnifying lenses inserted in frames were used for reading in Europe and China at about the same time, apparently; and it is a matter of controversy whether the West learned from the East or vice versa. In Europe, glasses first appeared in Italy. [...] The first portrait to show eyeglasses is that of Hugh of Provence by Tommaso da Modena, painted at Treviso in 1352. In 1480, Domenico Ghirlandaio painted St. Jerome at a desk from which dangled eyeglasses; as a result of the portrait, St. Jerome became the patron saint of the spectacles makers' guild.

The earliest glasses were convex lenses, which aided farsightedness. A concave lens for myopia, or nearsightedness, is first evident in the portrait of Pope Leo X painted by Raphael in 1517.

In 1784, Benjamin Franklin invented bifocals, dividing his lenses for distant and near vision, the split parts being held together by the frame. [...]

Originally lenses were made of transparent quartz and beryl, but increased demand led to the adoption of optical glass, for which Venice and Nürnberg were the chief centers. [...]

Extracted from: Encyclopaedia Britannica, 15th edition, 1974 – Micropaedia, volume IV, page 16.

Printing press

[...] The earliest mention of a printing press is in a lawsuit in Strasbourg in 1439 revealing construction of a press for Johann Gutenberg and his associates. The invention obviously owed much to the medieval paper press, in turn modeled after the ancient wine-and-olive press of the Mediterranean area. [...]

Metal presses began to appear late in the 18th century, at about which time the advantages of the cylinder were first perceived and consideration was given to the application of steam power. By mid-19th century, Richard M. Hoe of New York had perfected a power-driven cylinder press in which large central cylinders carrying the type successively printed on the paper of four impression cylinders, producing 8,000 sheets an hour by 2,000 revolutions.

Extracted from: Encyclopaedia Britannica, 15th edition, 1974 – Micropaedia, volume VIII, pages 218-19.

UNCOVERING THE *TEXT*

TOPIC

____

GENRE

What kind of texts are the ones on pages 50 and 51?

- ☐ article
- ☐ encyclopedia entries
- ☐ biography
- ☐ form

Scanning is a reading strategy!

Passar os olhos pelo texto de forma detalhada em busca de informações específicas ajuda-nos a encontrar caminhos para compreender o texto.

RELATED LINKS

For more information on this Link's topics, please visit:

http://www.medievalists.net/
http://medieval.stormthecastle.com/medieval-jobs.htm

FORUM

How can inventions benefit or harm humanity?

What are some things that, in your opinion, still need to be invented?

1 What are some of the characteristics of an encyclopedia entry?

1. Presents facts, well organized, has no relation with time. ☐
2. Presents opinions, well organized, has no relation with time. ☐
3. Presents facts, well organized, needs to be frequently updated. ☐

2 Read the first paragraph and answer the questions.

1. How long did the Middle Ages last?
____
2. When did the Middle Ages start?
____
3. Which part of the Middle Ages is considered the Dark Ages?
____

3 Scan the entry about eyeglasses and say what the dates and names refer to.

1. Italy: ______________________
2. Hugh of Provence: ______________________
3. Treviso: ______________________
4. 1352: ______________________
5. Domenico Ghirlandaio: ______________________
6. Pope Leo X: ______________________
7. 1517: ______________________
8. 1784: ______________________

4 Read the entry about the spinning wheel and check the correct sentences.

1. There is no certainty as to where it was invented. ☐
2. It was not invented in Europe. ☐
3. The British improved it. ☐

EXPANDING THE *VOCABULARY*

1 Find a word or expression in the text that means:

1. break down, fall ("Middle Ages" introduction): ________________
2. inactive ("Middle Ages" introduction): ________________
3. hang or swing loosely ("Eyeglasses" entry): ________________
4. helped ("Eyeglasses" entry): ________________
5. most important, main ("Eyeglasses" entry): ________________

2 What do the following chunks of language mean? Choose the best alternative.

1. ...owed much to the medieval paper press, *in turn* modeled after the ancient wine-and-olive press...
   a. em torno ☐ b. por sua vez ☐ c. tornando-se ☐
2. ...the split parts being *held together* by the frame.
   a. coladas ao mesmo tempo ☐ c. grudadas com cola ☐
   b. mantidas juntas ☐
3. ...the individual fibers were *drawn out* of a mass of wool held on a stick...
   a. retirados ☐ b. desembaraçados ☐ c. desligados ☐

3 What is the function of the following linking words?

1. ...as the Middle Ages, *and* the first half of...
   a. adicionar informações ☐
   b. contrastar ideias ☐
   c. questionar ideias ☐
2. ...quartz and beryl, *but* increased demand led to the adoption of...
   a. contrastar ideias ☐
   b. questionar ideias ☐
   c. adicionar ideias ☐
3. ...invented in India, *though* its origins are obscure.
   a. contrastar duas ou mais ideias ☐
   b. adicionar uma ideia ☐
   c. introduzir uma ideia diferente ☐

Linking Words

Linking words ou *connectors* são usados para dar coerência e coesão aos textos.

adicionar ideias	contrastar ideias	alternativa
and	but	or
also	however	either... or
as well as	on the contrary	
furthermore	in contrast	
in addition	on the other hand	
	although	

4 Choose the correct linking word.

1. ______________ to the party they had last year, this one is great.
   a. Contraryly ☐ b. In contrast ☐ c. On the contrary ☐
2. I do not agree that his latest album is bad. ______________, I find it one of his best.
   a. In contrast ☐ b. But ☐ c. On the contrary ☐
3. It is clear that the situation in Brazil will improve. ______________, the economic problems being experienced by most of the population will be sorted out.
   a. Also ☐ b. Or ☐ c. And ☐
4 I'm not going out tonight, ______________ I can see you tomorrow if you are free.
   a. although ☐ b. however ☐ c. but ☐
5. In order to try to reduce car use in cities, the government has announced new restrictions on car parking spaces ______________ a new tax on individual car use.
   a. also ☐ b. and ☐ c. however ☐

5 Take a look at the following sentences. There are two words with the same suffix. What are they and what is the suffix?

The earliest glasses were convex lenses, which aided farsightedness. A concave lens for myopia, or nearsightedness, is first evident in the portrait of Pope Leo X painted by Raphael in 1517.

____

6 Add the suffix *-ness* to the following words and use them to complete the sentences.

Suffix *ness*

O sufixo ***-ness*** transforma adjetivos em substantivos e significa justamente o estado caracterizado pelo adjetivo que dá origem a esse substantivo.

1. dark: ______________	5. helpful: ______________
2. happy: ______________	6. kind: ______________
3. forgetful: ______________	7. sad: ______________
4. forgive: ______________	8. lazy: ______________

1. Usually, ______________ is scary for children. They prefer leaving at least a dim glow of a light bulb on.
2. All that ______________ in serving us left a great impression about the restaurant.
3. ______________ is part of a teenager's life. You hardly see a teen who doesn't like a long night's sleep.
4. She couldn't keep all that ______________ inside her. She had to tell everybody the great news.

DISCOVERING *GRAMMAR*

Simple Past – Regular verbs

It is a matter of controversy whether the West *learned* from the East or vice versa.

Simple Past: Expressa hábitos, ações ou situações que ocorreram em determinado tempo no passado e já se encerraram. No passado, não há diferença de conjugação conforme o pronome. Para formar o *Simple Past*, usamos: sujeito + verbo no passado + complemento

I *lived* in the country two years ago.

He *studied* hard when they *were* young.

Grande parte dos verbos obedecem a um mesmo padrão ao ser usados no passado, assim sendo, são chamados regulares. Preste atenção à tabela:

Base form	Past form
invent	invented
increase	increased
insert	inserted

Base form	Past form
learn	learned
paint	painted
aid	aided

A terminação *-d/-ed* se repete em todos eles. Logo, todos os verbos que recebem essa terminação quando no passado, são regulares:

In Europe, glasses fisrt *appeared* in Italy.

In 1784, Benjamin Franklin *invented* bifocals.

Para frases negativas e interrogativas, precisamos usar o auxiliar *do* em sua forma no passado: *did*. As mesmas regras do *Simple Present* se aplicam. Note que, quando há o uso do verbo auxiliar, o verbo principal volta à ***base form***.

Negative form: sujeito + *did* + *not* + verbo (*base form*) + complemento

Interrogative form: *did* + sujeito + verbo (*base form*) + complemento

Alguns advérbios e expressões de tempo são comumente associados com o ***Simple Past***:

yesterday, last week/month/year, some years/months/hours ago, in January/March..., etc.

Spelling: verb + d/ed

A maioria dos verbos recebe ***-ed*** sem sofrer modificações:

*play – play**ed*** *talk – talk**ed***
*enjoy – enjoy**ed***

E verbos terminados em *e* recebem apenas ***-d***:

like – lik***ed*** live – liv***ed***

Mas, ao receberem ***-ed***, os verbos terminados em sílaba tônica formada de consoante + vogal + consoante dobram a consoante:

*stop – sto**pped***
*occur – occu**rred***
*rob – ro**bbed***
*admit – admi**tted***
*prefer – prefe**rred***
*permit – permi**tted***

Nos verbos terminados em consoante + ***y***, muda-se o ***y*** para ***i***:

*carry – carr**ied***
*study – stud**ied***
*hurry – hurr**ied***

1 **Write down all the regular verbs in the past in the "Eyeglasses" entry.**

Communication Bytes

1 **Jeff and Ron are talking about their weekend. Listen to the conversation and answer T for *true*, F for *false*, or NS for *not stated*.** (15)

1. Jeff invited Ron to an exposition. ☐
2. Jeff learned a lesson. ☐
3. The exposition was really crowded. ☐
4. Jeff's phone was off. ☐
5. Jeff is interested in the Middle Ages. ☐
6. Jeff stayed at home during the weekend. ☐

2 **What kind of things do you usually do during your weekends? Number the following in order of preference from 1 (the most interesting) to 7 (the least interesting).**

wash the car

watch TV

walk the dog

study

play sports

visit relatives

talk on the phone

LANGUAGE HELP

I played… on Saturday afternoon.

We played … in the evening / morning / afternoon.

She… at night.

3 **Now talk to a partner about your last weekend. You can use some of the actions in the dialogue and in exercise 2.**

Linked Skills

1 **Do you happen to know who invented some of the objects we use nowadays? No? Don't worry! Listen to this report and match the names and dates to the inventions.** (16)

WHO				
Asians	Roger L. Easton	Sumerians and Egyptians	François de Rivaz	Eugene Polley

WHEN				
3000BC	1806	5000 years ago	1955	about 50 years ago

WHAT				
				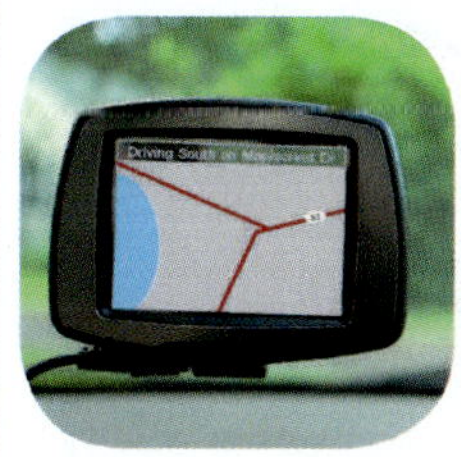

2 **Now use the information to write about the inventions below. You can use the transcript of the previous exercise to help you.**

Disposable diapers:
Marion Donovan, 1949;
patented in 1951

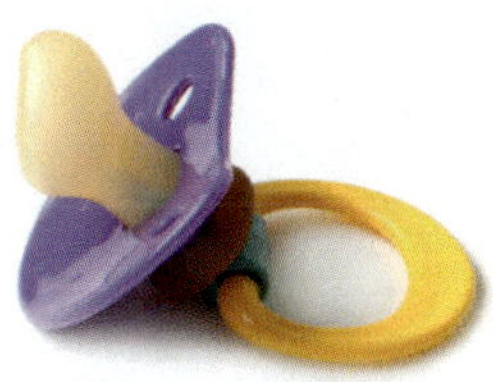

Pacifier:
Sears Roebuck
USA, 1902

Plastic: Leo Hendrik
Baekeland, 1909

Medieval Jesters

17

Facts and interesting information about Medieval Life, specifically, Medieval Jesters

[...] A Jester is a professional clown employed to entertain a king or nobleman in the Middle Ages. Also referred to as a fool, buffoon or clown. The Medieval jesters [...] can be compared to the circus clowns of today. The class of professional court jesters reached its culminating point of influence and recognized place and function in the social organism during the Middle Ages.

[...] Medieval Jesters played a minor role in court life but certainly brightened up the entertainments. The history of court jesters dated back before the Medieval era of the Middle Ages, which they are most closely associated with. Medieval jesters were responsible for bringing a smile to the face of a monarch who was feeling angry or who was feeling unwell. The role of the Medieval jester was to amuse his master, to excite him to laughter by sharp contrast, to prevent the over-oppression of state affairs, and, in harmony with a well-known physiological precept, by his liveliness at meals to assist his lord's digestion.

[...] The clothing of Medieval court jesters – what did they wear? The heads of Medieval jesters were shaved, their coats were motley and the breeches tight, with generally one leg different in color from the other. The head was covered with a garment resembling a monk's cowl, which fell over the breast and shoulders. The first Medieval jesters wore a hat depicting the ears of an ass – the ass's tail was then added to his costume. The clothes worn by the court jester moved on to gaudy, brightly colored, and humorous attire. The Medieval jester's cloth hat, called a Fool's hat, was most distinctive, consisting of three points with a jingle bell at the end of each point. A court jester would also carry a mock sceptre, called a bauble, which was adorned by a carved head or the inflated bladder of an animal.

[...] The Medieval Jester held privileges which were not afforded to many other persons at court. The court jester was one of the few characters in the court who could freely speak his mind without causing offence and somebody who could use humor to mock, jibe, and joke about the lords, ladies and nobles of the court. Jesters came from a wide variety of backgrounds, and many of them were well educated. The predecessors of the Medieval jesters were the jongleurs, and some jesters were recruited from this band of entertainers.

Extracted from: www.medieval-life-and-times.info/medieval-life/medieval-jesters.htm

Think about it!

How important is comedy for our lives?
What or who plays the role of a jester in your life—TV, friends, books, the Internet, movies?

Reading Comprehension

1 **Read the text and match the titles to the paragraphs.**

paragraph 1	☐ clothing
paragraph 2	☐ definition
paragraph 3	☐ freedom of speech
paragraph 4	☐ role

2 **Find three synonyms of *jester*.**

____

3 **Find three synonyms of *make fun of*.**

____

4 **Find the words on page 59 that mean:**

1. make something more pleasant (line 2) – ________________
2. king (line 6) – ________________
3. entertain (line 7) – ________________
4. government activities (line 9) – ________________
5. instruction (line 10) – ________________
6. trousers (line 14) – ________________
7. similar (line 16) – ________________
8. flashy, brilliant, colorful (line 20) – ________________
9. clothes (line 20) – ________________

5 **Read the text and complete the sentences with information from the text.**

1. Jesters were ________________ clowns.
2. They were expected to ____________________________.
3. They could say ________________________ and nobody punished them.
4. They held ________________ which were not afforded to other people.
5. They came from a variety of __________________.
6. The ________________ of medieval jesters were shaved.

Hyperlinks

inventions + imagination

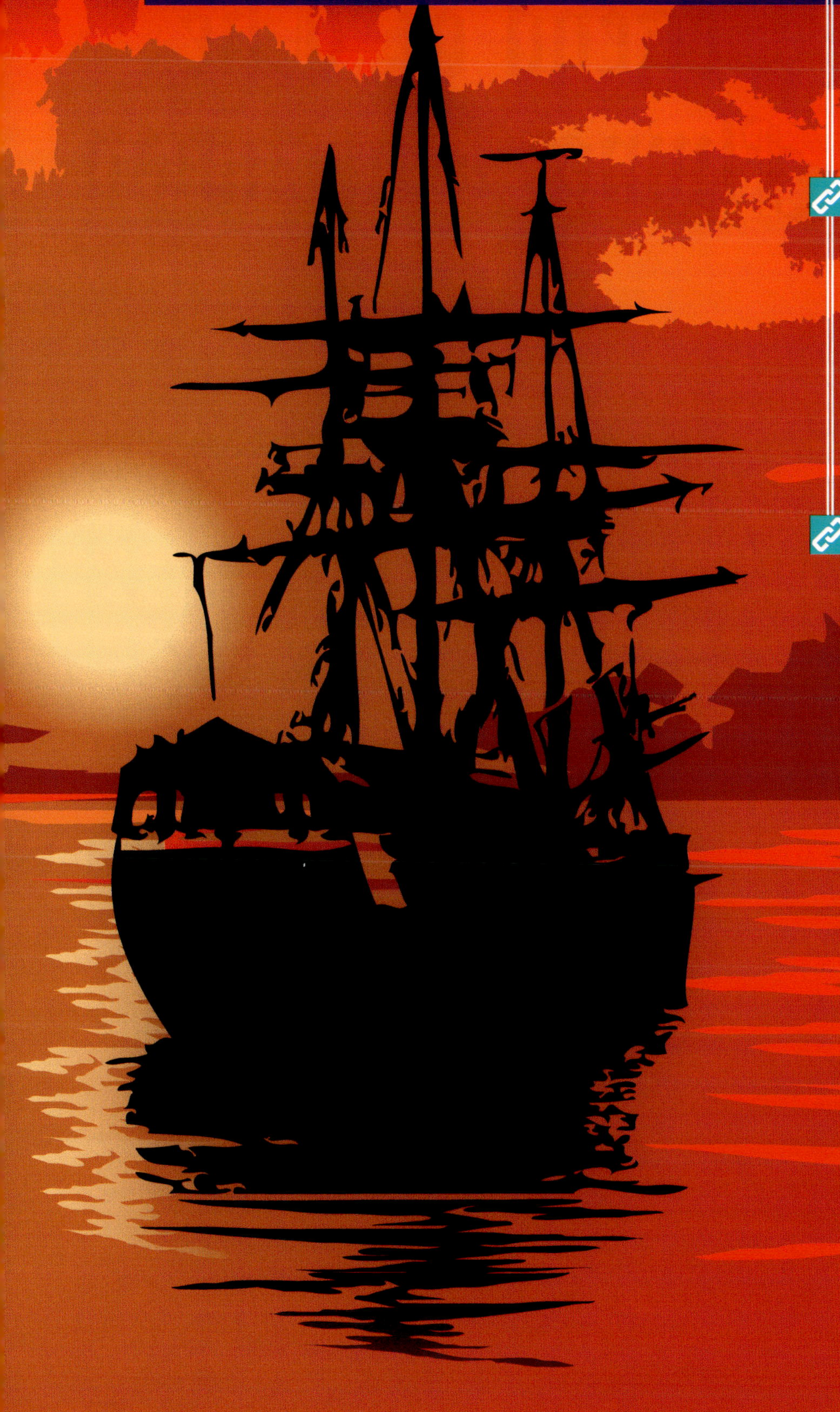

Legend of The Flying Dutchman

By James Donahue

LOG IN

1 Do you believe in legends?

2 Do you know of any Brazilian legends?

WORD BANK

crew: tripulação
cursed: amaldiçoada
devil: diabo
gale: vento muito violento
legend: lenda
rigging: cordame
uncanny: estranho

NOTES

[...]

This ghost story has its origins in both Dutch and German legend. The most common is a tale about a Captain Hendrick Vanderdecken, who set sail in 1680 from Amsterdam to Batavia, in the Dutch East Indies, and disappeared in a gale while rounding the Cape [of Good Hope].

It is said that Vanderdecken ignored the danger and pressed on into the teeth of the tempest. The ship foundered, sending all aboard to their deaths. As punishment for his foolishness, Vanderdecken and his ship are doomed to spend eternity fighting the tempest at the Cape.

[...] There is a second version of the story. This one tells of a Captain Bernard Fokke, who was known for the uncanny speed of his trips from Holland to Java, and people said he was in league with the devil.

[...] In all of the stories, the ship remains unnamed. The reference to the "Flying Dutchman" appears to describe the cursed captain and not the ship.

According to most versions, the captain refuses to retreat in the face of the storm. In yet other stories, some terrible crime occurs on the ship, or the crew is struck by the plague and is not allowed to enter any port. For whatever the reason, the ship and its crew are doomed to sail forever.

[...] While there is general agreement that the Lost Dutchman is merely a legend, there have been actual reported sightings of a 17th-century sailing ship battling the elements at the Cape of Good Hope over the years.

Perhaps the first officially reported sighting occurred in 1835, when a crew of a British ship was rounding the cape and observed a "phantom ship" approaching in the shroud of a severe storm. The British crew said the vessel appeared to be on a collision course, but then it suddenly vanished.

The H.M.S. Bacchante encountered the Flying Dutchman again in 1881, also at the cape. The following day, one of the two men that made the sighting fell to his death from the rigging, thus enhancing the story to include a curse on those that see the ghostly vessel.

A more recent sighting was made by people on the shore in March, 1939. What was astounding was that it was seen by dozens of people who all gave a detailed description of a Dutch merchantman from the 17th century.

The last recorded sighting occurred at Cape Town in 1942, when four witnesses saw a sailing ship enter Table Bay and then disappear before their eyes.

Extracted from: http://perdurabo10.tripod.com/ships/id19.html

UNCOVERING THE *TEXT*

TOPIC

____

GENRE

What kind of text is on pages 62 and 63?

- [ ] blog entry
- [ ] encyclopedia entry
- [ ] quiz
- [ ] article

Looking for what pronouns refer to is a reading strategy!

Identificar a que os pronomes se referem num texto ajuda a compreendê-lo melhor, evitando que o leitor se confunda sobre o que está sendo abordado naquele momento.

RELATED LINKS

For more information on this Link's topics, please visit:

http://myths.e2bn.org/
http://www.ghostship-softheworld.com/

FORUM

How can myths and folk tales benefit society?

1 What do the underlined words refer to?

1. ...punishment for <u>his</u> foolishness... (line 7)
____
2. This <u>one</u> tells of a... (line 9)
____
3. ...include a curse on <u>those</u> that see... (line 27)
____
4. ...was that <u>it</u> was seen by... (line 30)
____
5. ...disappear before <u>their</u> eyes. (line 37)
____

2 Scan the text and say what the following dates and places refer to.

1. Amsterdam – ___________________________
2. 1680 – ___________________________
3. Cape Town – ___________________________
____
4. 1835 – ___________________________
5. 1881 – ___________________________

3 Choose the correct alternative.

1. The text can be classified as a narrative because...
   a. it states facts about a certain legend. [ ]
   b. it presents a chronological sequence. [ ]
2. The author of the text...
   a. believes in the legend of the Flying Dutchman. [ ]
   b. does not state his personal opinion about the story. [ ]
3. According to the author's research,
   a. there are some facts that lead people to believe the legend is true. [ ]
   b. lots of people believe in the legend. [ ]

EXPANDING THE *VOCABULARY*

1 Choose the best translation for the following language chunks.

1. ...pressed on into the teeth of the tempest... (lines 5 and 6)
   a. pressionado pela tempestade ☐ c. continuou em direção à tempestade ☐
   b. com os dentes rangendo pela tempestade ☐
2. ...in league with the devil... (line 11)
   a. na liga do diabo ☐ b. aliado ao diabo. ☐ c. alinhado com o diabo ☐
3. ...battling the elements... (line 19)
   a. batalhando pelos elementos ☐ c. lutando contra a natureza ☐
   b. lutando contra os componentes ☐
4. ...in the shroud of a severe storm... (lines 22 and 23)
   a. envolto em forte tempestade. ☐ c. no meio da terrível tempestade. ☐
   b. no manto da tempestade ☐

2 Find a word that means...

1. story, legend (paragraph 1): ______________________________
2. sank (paragraph 2): ______________________________
3. sentenced, condemned (paragraph 2): ____________________
4. continues (paragraph 4): ______________________________

3 Look at the words taken from the text and choose the one that is not a synonym.

1. struck (line 15)
   a. hit ☐ b. beat ☐ c. slap ☐ d. punish ☐
2. plague (line 15)
   a. epidemic ☐ b. contagious ☐ c. disease ☐ d. pest ☐
3. merely (line 18)
   a. just ☐ b. only ☐ c. entirely ☐ d. simply ☐
4. actual (line 19)
   a. today ☐ b. concrete ☐ c. real ☐ d. exact ☐
5. vessel (line 27)
   a. ship ☐ b. boat ☐ c. vase ☐ d. watercraft ☐
6. astounding (line 30)
   a. assuring ☐ b. amazing ☐ c. stunning ☐ d. surprising ☐

4 **In the sentence "It is said that Vanderdecken ignored the danger and pressed on into the teeth of the tempest," the phrasal verb *press on* means to continue doing something, to continue moving forward. Look at other phrasal verbs with *on* and choose the best translation for each of them, according to the context.**

1. We don't *get on* very well. I don't like her!
   a. dar-se bem com alguém ☐
   b. conversar ☐
2. Just *hang on* for a second. I need to answer this phone call.
   a. segurar algo ☐
   b. esperar ☐
3. *Put* your coat *on* because it's cold outside.
   a. colocar em cima ☐
   b. vestir ☐
4. His younger brother usually *told on* him when he did something wrong.
   a. dedurar ☐
   b. dar bronca ☐

5 **In the sentence "The reference to the 'Flying Dutchman' appears to describe the cursed captain and not the ship," the word *cursed* is a verb used as an adjective. Find other verbs used as adjectives in the following sentences and circle them.**

1. I can't resist his smiling face. It's just so cute!
2. I still didn't have the chance to visit that recently recommended restaurant.
3. We need the translated version of this book. The original is in Russian!
4. Well, sometimes it's better to buy a used one.
5. That singing bird wakes up really early!

Para serem usados como adjetivos, os verbos estão geralmente no particípio presente ou particípio passado. Por exemplo, *talking* ***robot***, *lost* ***wallet***, *cursed* **captain**. Para os verbos regulares, o particípio passado tem o mesmo formato do *Simple Past*.

Simple Past – Irregular Verbs

...1942, when four witnesses *saw* a sailing ship...
The British crew *said* the vessel appeared to be on a collision course...

Os verbos que seguem o padrão de acrescentar *–ed* ao final da palavra para formar a *past form* são chamados regulares. Entretanto, existem verbos que não seguem esse mesmo padrão e que, por isso, são chamados *irregulares*. Os verbos irregulares não têm regra fixa para a forma do passado:

Base form	Past form
see	saw
say	said

Sua forma segue os mesmos padrões do *Simple Past* com verbos regulares. A diferença está em que, repetimos, o *Past Form* não segue um mesmo padrão.

Form:

Affirmative: She *swam* yesterday.
subject + verb (past form) + complement

Interrogative: *Did* she *swim* yesterday?
auxiliary (past form) + subject + verb (base form) + complement

Negative: She *did not* *swim* yesterday.
subject + auxiliary + verb (base form) + complement
verb (past form) + not

In wh- questions: What *did* you *buy* yesterday? Where *did* he *drive*?

Apesar de não seguirem um padrão fixo, existem alguns grupos com formas próximas. Veja alguns exemplos:

cut – cut	think – thought	run – ran	drive – drove	make – made	sleep – slept
put–put	buy–bought	ring–rang	write–wrote	pay–paid	keep–kept

1 Underline all the Simple Past irregular verbs in the sentence.

The following day, one of the two men that made the sighting fell to his death from the rigging...

2 Complete the sentences with the Simple Past of the verbs in parentheses. If you need help, check the "Irregular Verbs" list at the end of your book.

1. She ______________ (leave) home early today.
2. I ______________ (take) the bus because my father's car ______________ (break) down.
3. It ______________ (cost) a fortune.
4. The mail ______________ (come) yesterday.
5. My father only ______________ (drink) soda because he ______________ (have) to drive us home.

Writing Bits

A Story

1 **Read the story and number the pictures according to the narrated events.**

19

It Happened to Me

This is a true story. One cold dark night, I was driving along a quiet country road when I heard a noise. Suddenly, the car skidded, and I had to hold the steering wheel firmly not to lose control. I slowed down and stopped the car. I sat inside it for a couple of minutes.

I got out of the car and realized that one of the front tires was flat. I must confess that I do not know how to change a tire. There I was alone, without a phone, and without anyone in sight. Suddenly, I saw a shadow in the distance. It seemed to be walking towards me. I waved and shouted. When the man got close to me, I said, "You are the answer to my prayers! Could you please help me change the tire? I don't know how to do it." He just nodded and changed the tire. After that, he walked away. I got back into the car and drove home.

The following day at work, I told my friends what had happened. They were surprised. The man could have been a robber. He could have attacked me. I could have been killed. It was only then that I realized how lucky I had been.

2 **Write your own story. Include when and where it happened, who was involved, what exactly happened, and how it all ended. You can use words from the box below. Use from 100 to 300 words.**

first then after that suddenly later
the following day / week finally

Review

1 **Read the sentences about Christopher Columbus, a famous and successful sailor, and check the correct past tense form.**

1. Columbus ______________ in several expeditions to Africa.
   a. participated ☐ b. participates ☐ c. is going to participate ☐
2. In 1492, Columbus ______________ Spain in the *Santa Maria*, with the *Pinta* and the *Niña* alongside.
   a. lived ☐ b. leave ☐ c. left ☐
3. His first voyage into the Atlantic Ocean, in 1476, nearly ______________ him his life.
   a. cost ☐ b. costs ☐ c. costed ☐
4. For a while, he ______________ a commercial fleet. It was at that time that some French privateers attacked him off the coast of Portugal.
   a. sail ☐ b. sailed ☐ c. sold ☐
5. He ______________ the distance between the Canary Islands and Japan to be about 2,300 miles.
   a. is estimating ☐ b. estimated ☐ c. was estimated ☐
6. Columbus and his crewmen visited some islands where the natives ______________ bits of gold for adornment.
   a. wearing ☐ b. weared ☐ c. wore ☐
7. He ______________ on May 20th, 1506, believing he had discovered a shorter route to Asia.
   a. died ☐ b. dead ☐ c. death ☐
8. Some people blame Columbus for the destruction of the native peoples of the islands he ______________.
   a. exploration ☐ b. exploring ☐ c. explored ☐

Source: www.biography.com/people/christopher-columbus-9254209?page=3

2 **Complete the text with the Simple Past of the verbs in the box.**

1. have	2. refuse	3. abandon	4. be	5. float

20

Baychimo

Arctic Ghost Ship
by Anthony Dalton

No vessel that sailed the Arctic seas has raised so much speculation or triggered imaginations as has the legendary Hudson's Bay Company ship *Baychimo*.

[...]

This ship's story [1] ________________ a remarkable twist. Caught in 1931 in an ice floe that [2] ________________ to let go, her crew expected her to sink at any moment and [3] ________________ ship. But Baychimo [4] ________________ as stubborn as the ice, and she [5] ________________ away unharmed to begin what would prove to be the longest phase of her seemingly charmed career: for the next four decades, she would appear on the horizon at unexpected times and places, always defiantly upright and afloat, becoming the legendary ghost ship of the Arctic.

Extracted from: www.hgdistribution.com/book_details.php?isbn_upc=9781894974141

3 Answer the questions.

1. What does the pronoun *that* refer to in the sentence "No vessel that sailed the Arctic seas…"?

____

2. What does the pronoun *that* refer to in the sentence "Caught in 1931 in an ice floe that refused to let go…"?

____

4 Identify the sentences as T for *true* or F for *false*.

1. The text is about a ghost ship because people believe there were ghosts in it. ☐
2. The ship got caught in lots of ice and couldn't move. ☐
3. The crew thought it would sink, so they abandoned ship. ☐
4. The ship sank in the middle of the ocean right after the crew abandoned it. ☐
5. The ship still floated around for forty years. ☐

5 Check the correct meaning or translation.

1. …she floated away unharmed…
   - a. ela flutuou sem se machucar ☐
   - b. o barco saiu flutuando sem danos ☐
   - c. ela flutuou para fora sem machucados ☐
2. …always defiantly upright and afloat…

   Upright and *afloat* mean
   - a. aprumado e flutuando. ☐
   - b. direito e afundando. ☐
   - c. para cima e ao lado. ☐
3. …has raised so much speculation or triggered imaginations...
   - a. aumentou a especulação ou despertou imaginações ☐
   - b. causou tanta especulação ou despertou o imaginário coletivo ☐
   - c. tem aumentado tanta especulação ou ativado imaginação ☐
4. …at unexpected times and places...
   - a. em desesperador tempos e lugares ☐
   - b. em inesperador tempos e lugares ☐
   - c. em horários e locais inesperados ☐

So far, SO GOOD?

1 **Find the verbs in the box in the Simple Past form.**

send   go   cry   happen   cut   think
teach   run   swim   give   write   fall

D	E	N	E	P	P	A	H	U	F	T	M	C	A	S
H	C	Y	G	A	V	E	T	Z	E	F	P	R	C	I
C	A	U	G	H	T	H	K	S	L	E	R	I	T	F
L	T	S	O	C	G	H	D	O	T	L	K	E	H	Y
M	I	U	M	U	D	T	G	A	P	H	B	D	G	R
W	Q	A	O	R	P	F	S	U	E	S	I	Z	U	A
I	D	B	A	E	E	D	T	O	O	R	R	T	O	N
E	K	N	L	L	W	U	I	Z	L	H	X	J	R	Q
T	K	S	L	K	C	B	A	A	M	D	T	M	B	W
O	A	A	P	X	T	E	W	M	S	L	M	U	C	N
E	W	U	C	S	E	N	T	E	D	I	A	P	X	E
T	J	X	G	E	V	O	R	D	N	P	W	R	M	T
O	M	N	M	H	P	U	T	W	U	T	S	A	M	O
R	S	E	D	R	T	A	V	T	J	R	O	Y	S	L
W	T	W	J	P	R	F	Q	U	E	M	A	C	M	D

2 **Unscramble the words to form sentences.**

1. often / or / legend / brave / about / adventures / a / is / people

   ____

2. or / work / a / people / on / plane / all / that / crew / the / are / together / ship

   ____

3. of / the / is / the / in / nineteenth / movie / real / a / portrait / life / century

   ____

Now that I've finished links 5 and 6, I can…

…use verbs in the Simple Past.	☐ Yes!	☐ I still need to study more!
…ask and answer questions in the Simple Past.	☐ Yes!	☐ I still need to study more!
…tell stories.	☐ Yes!	☐ I still need to study more!
…narrate events.	☐ Yes!	☐ I still need to study more!

Hyperlinks

food + health

LINK 7

Eating Disorders

Communication Bytes

Linked Skills

World Links

LINK 8

Nutrition Facts

LINK 7

LOG IN

1 What are eating disorders?

2 What causes them?

3 Do you know of anyone who has faced this problem?

WORD BANK

calf: panturrilha
crest: brasão
failure: fracasso
fears: medos
intersecting: cruzados
lacrosse: jogo de bola com raquetes e duas equipes de dez jogadores
sticks: tacos

NOTES

I Chose to Live

[...]

My life looked quite ideal on the outside, and I seemingly coasted through my high school years. I set numerous records in lacrosse, football, and weightlifting during my four years of school, and I always had the "popular" girlfriend. I used these superficial achievements and model relationships to create a false and unhealthy identity. Nothing could touch me, and I made myself believe that I was invincible. I even went so far as to get a tattoo of the Superman crest on my calf with intersecting lacrosse sticks.

This Superman type of mentality carried me through the first twenty-one years of my life, but eventually the walls I had falsely built came tumbling down in the form of depression, substance abuse, and Anorexia Nervosa. The word "failure" was not a part of my life, nor did I believe that I would ever fail in anything. With this unrealistic type of thinking, I was setting myself up like a ticking time bomb – inevitably things would explode all around me!

[...]

Feeling rejuvenated from therapy, I raced back out on my own chasing "perfection." I got my girlfriend back, found a great job, and seven months later I was engaged. I spent much of 2007 working and planning the wedding. On the outside I looked happier than ever, but I was suffering emotionally on the inside. I kept this front up until March of 2008, and my body just couldn't take it anymore. I needed an intervention of sort and got just that. The hardest thing for me to do was ask for help, but it was the best decision I ever made.

[...]

Riding on pure adrenalin, I spent two straight weeks researching treatment. It was a difficult process because, at this time, there weren't many programs that took men. I finally found a center that met my needs and I was on a plane two days later. I spent thirty days separating myself from my eating disorder. I was taught to see my ED as a separate person and used various types of therapy to uncover my true identity. The shocking thing that I learned was that eating disorders aren't about food – it's about trauma, feelings, emotions, low self-esteem, and fears.

[...]

Treatment gave me an amazing foundation into my recovery and rebuilding my life. It has been more than a year since doctors told me I had less than twelve months to live. I am now a completely different and healthy person. My road to recovery hasn't been perfect, but nothing ever is. I have learned to embrace adversity and to learn from my mistakes.

[...]

Eating disorders don't discriminate and neither does recovery – there is HOPE, and you're never alone in this. If you are suffering from an ED, please reach out and get help! To read my full story and learn more about my outreach, please visit www.ichosetolive.com.

"Together we can make it through somehow."

I Chose To Live and Choose To Care!

Patrick Bergstrom

Mission – Eliminate Eating Disorders!
patrickb@ichosetolive.com

Extracted from: www.nationaleatingdisorders.org/information-resources/story-of-hope-detail.php?story=5&title=I%20chose

UNCOVERING THE *TEXT*

TOPIC

____

GENRE

What kind of text is the one on page 75?

- [ ] fiction
- [ ] testimonial
- [ ] graph
- [ ] article

Identifying topics is a reading strategy!

Quando conseguimos identificar o tópico abordado em cada parágrafo, obtemos uma visão global do texto que nos ajuda a compreendê-lo.

RELATED LINKS

For more information on this Link's topics, please visit:

http://visual.ly/eating-weight-disorders

http://eat-26.com/Form/index.php

FORUM

Why are there so many eating-related problems (anorexia, bulimia, obesity, etc.) and how can you help people who suffer from them?

How can a person avoid being caught in such disorders?

1 Read the text and match the topics to the paragraphs.

paragraph 1	[ ] health problems
paragraph 2	[ ] getting help
paragraph 3	[ ] present state
paragraph 4	[ ] school
paragraph 5	[ ] advice
paragraph 6	[ ] recovery and plea for help

2 Rewrite the statements below to make them correct according to the text.

1. Patrick led a perfect life when he was at school.

____

2. He realized he had been cheating himself soon after he graduated.

____

3. While he was planning his wedding, he realized he couldn't go on pretending.

____

4. Treatment taught him to separate personal life from his problems.

____

5. He has recovered from all the mistakes.

____

3 Answer the following questions.

1. What made him realize he needed help?

____

2. What sort of advice does he give people who face the same problem?

____

EXPANDING THE *VOCABULARY*

1 Choose the correct translation for the following italicized chunks.

1. "…I *seemingly coasted through* my high school years." (lines 2 and 3)
   a. aparentemente fui bem-sucedido ☐ c. tive problemas parecidos ☐
   b. passei bons anos ☐
2. "…falsely built, *came tumbling down* in the form of…" (lines 15 and 16)
   a. desabou ☐ b. caiu no chão ☐ c. veio caindo pra baixo ☐
3. "…I spent two *straight* weeks…" (lines 35 and 36)
   a. retas ☐ b. sem parar ☐ c. em uma direção ☐
4. "…learn more about my *outreach*,…" (lines 61 and 62)
   a. alcance ☐ b. programa de ajuda ☐ c. problema ☐

2 Match the words to the synonyms or definitions.

1. achievements (line 7)	☐ encircle, seize, hug
2. crest (line 11)	☐ find out about something that was hidden
3. eventually (line 15)	☐ something someone completed successfully
4. uncover (line 43)	☐ at the end of a process or period of time
5. foundation (line 49)	☐ design used as the symbol of a family
6. embrace (line 55)	☐ basis

3 In the sentence, "I was setting myself up like a ticking time bomb – inevitably things would explode all around me!" we have the phrasal verb *set up*. Check out some other phrasal verbs with *set* and choose the correct meaning based on their use in these sentences.

1. Although there was a lot of proof against him, the criminal said the police *set* him *up* and that he was innocent.
   a. fazer uma armação, enganar alguém ☐ c. dar meios para alguém fazer algo ☐
   b. organizar ☐
2. They *set out* on a dangerous journey across the country, but I've heard they are already halfway through it.
   a. organizar ☐ b. partir numa jornada ☐ c. ser bem-sucedido em algo ☐
3. These books are *set apart* for donation.
   a. retirar de algum lugar ☐ b. distanciar ☐ c. separar com um propósito ☐
4. My alarm clock *sets off* at six in the morning.
   a. começar a tocar, ativar ☐ b. desligar, parar de funcionar ☐ c. organizar ☐

4 **Look at the following sentence: "I am now a completely different and healthy person." When we talk about a person that is completely different and healthy, we say "completely different and healthy person" because *completely different and healthy* are adjectives that describe the noun *person*. Now, choose the correct position for the following adjectives.**

1. The girl is nice and little.
   a. She is a girl nice and little. ☐ b. She is a nice little girl. ☐
2. Life has grips that are threatening.
   a. life grips threatening ☐ b. life-threatening grips ☐
3. His skin was puffy and pale.
   a. puffy and pale skin ☐ b. skin puffy and pale ☐
4. He was a strong baby. He was four months old.
   a. He was a strong four-month-old baby. ☐ b. He was a baby strong four months old. ☐

5 **Look at the following sentence: "I spent thirty days separating myself *from* my eating disorder." There are many uses for the preposition *from*. Number the sentences according to the use of the word *from* in each of them.**

1. Indicate a starting point of a physical movement, or a starting point in measuring or reckoning, or in a statement of limits.
2. Indicate the starting point of an activity.
3. Indicate physical separation or an act or condition of exclusion, subtraction, or differentiation.
4. Indicate the source, cause, agent, or basis.

☐ I was discouraged from participating.
☐ He's suffering from a very strong cold.
☐ This rug came from India. I bought it there last year.
☐ Summer in Paris goes from June until August.
☐ Summer courses will go from the tenth of January until the twentieth.
☐ The lions escaped from the Zoo.

6 **Underline all the nouns and adjectives with the *-ing* suffix from the text. Then put them in the correct column.**

Nouns	Adjectives

DISCOVERING *GRAMMAR*

Past Continuous

I *was setting* myself *up* like a ticking time bomb.
I *was suffering* emotionally on the inside.

Past Continuous: descreve ações em andamento em determinado momento do passado:

I *was sleeping* at 5 P.M.

I *was sleeping* when you arrived.

His cell phone rang while he *was studying*.

Para formarmos o *Past Continuous* em orações afirmativas, usamos: sujeito + verbo *to be* + verbo + *-ing*

Em orações negativas: sujeito + verbo *to be* + *not* + verbo + *-ing*

Em frases interrogativas: verbo *to be* + sujeito + verbo + *-ing*

Alguns advérbios e expressões de tempo são comumente associados com o *Past Continuous*. Por exemplo:

yesterday ago at in

1 Fill in the blanks with the Past Continuous of the verbs in parentheses.

1. The players ______________ (listen) to the coach's instructions.
2. We didn't have time to call you. We ______________ (organize) the event.
3. He ______________ (pay) for her gift when she walked into the store.
4. I ______________ (watch) TV, so I didn't hear the doorbell.
5. She ______________ (make) a sandwich when I arrived.
6. You ______________ (sleep) when I arrived, so I went home.

2 Answer the questions. Use the words in parentheses.

1. What were the boys doing? (swim)

____

2. What was Ann doing? (write a letter)

____

3. Was Joan playing the guitar? (no / sing)

____

4. What were they doing? (jog / park)

____

5. Were you sleeping? (no / watch a movie)

____

Communication Bytes

1 **Myriam is thinking about going on a diet. Listen to her conversation with Alison and answer**
22 **T for *true* or F for *false*.**

1. Myriam wants to go on a detox diet. ☐
2. Detox diets have only good aspects. ☐
3. Alison knows only good aspects of detox diets. ☐
4. Alison believes Myriam should see a doctor before going on a diet. ☐

2 **Look at the food pyramid and see part of Myriam's weekly lunch menu. Put a check (✓) on days her diet is correct and an *X* on days she should change it.**

Monday ☐
Rice Beans Lettuce and tomatoes Grilled chicken fillet Fresh fruit
Tuesday ☐
Gnocchi with white sauce
Wednesday ☐
Fish fillet Roast potato Cabbage Steamed carrots and green beans Fresh fruit

3 **Now talk to a partner about the advantages and disadvantages of going on a diet without a doctor's supervision. You can use some language from the box to help you.**

Introducing / adding ideas	Contrasting ideas	Reaching a conclusion
firstly secondly in addition	in comparison on the contrary on the one hand on the other hand however	in conclusion in short to conclude

Linked Skills

1 **Listen to an interview about a poll on organic foods and answer if the statements are T for *true* or F for *false*.** (23)

1. Most people prefer non-organic foods. ☐
2. Tiffany is responsible for the poll. ☐
3. People who are less than thirty-five years old would prefer organic food more frequently than older people. ☐
4. People end up buying non-organic food because it's cheaper than organic food. ☐
5. Most people are motivated by the taste of organic food when buying it. ☐

Source: www.factsforhealthcare.com/pressroom/NPR_report_OrganicFoods.pdf

2 **Write down three questions for an opinion poll about food (favorite kind of food, junk food versus healthy food, prices of food, etc.). Try using yes / no questions only. You can use the transcript on page 120 to help you.**

____

____

____

____

3 **Ask some of your colleagues to answer the questions you created and prepare the results using percentages.**

	Yes	No
Question 1	________%	________%
Question 2	________%	________%
Question 3	________%	________%

Eating Disorders:

Crispy fried chicken. Moist, gooey cake. Lobster ravioli smothered in cream sauce. These delectable foods might sound perfect to most people, but all over the world there are young girls who would turn down this food in a heartbeat because they have been persuaded to eat practically nothing in order to attain conventional beauty. Most people think eating disorders are simply a Western phenomenon, but I intend to show how they have begun to overtake the world. Eating disorders are rapidly spreading from the United States into other countries through culture and the media. Several scholars have their own views as to why eating disorders are becoming more globalized. While some focus on cultural and religious practices, others blame the media and new developments in technology that allow speedy, world-wide communication.

[...]

One example is the rise in the rates of eating disorders in European countries over the past few decades (Miller & Pumariega 99). In Hong Kong and India, anorexia is not induced by a desire to be thin, but rather for religious purposes or eccentric nutritional ideas (Miller & Pumariega 101).

Caroline Robinson

A Global Phenomenon

[...]

Today, doctors attribute the rise of eating disorders in Asia to the media as the use of diet pills and supplements increases drastically. Infomercials for weight-losing products are successfully convincing girls that they need diet pills to aid them in their quest to be thin (Efron, p. 1). The media is also playing a huge part in convincing young girls that they must be thin to be beautiful.

[...]

However, others argue from the perspective that eating disorders are socially constructed realities (Griffin 44). The people and media that a person is exposed to directly influence their opinions, rather than their decisions. Advertising plays a crucial role in the culture of consumption, and it plays a role in subtly changing consumer needs and channeling this desire into products.

[...]

Some experts argue that analyzing eating disorders in the context of globalization helps explain their increased prevalence in society and is also a key factor in overcoming the problems encountered in prevention and treatment (Edquist).

[...]

Source: www.lsu.edu/faculty/jwither/Essays/Health/Robinson_Essay.html

Think about it!

How much influence can media have on us?
What are other options for obtaining information or knowledge about a subject?

Reading Comprehension

1 Scan the text and match the statements to their authors.

1. Miller & Pumariega
2. Efron
3. Griffin
4. Edquist

☐ Eating disorders are socially constructed realities.

☐ Analyzing eating disorders in the context of globalization helps explain their predominance.

☐ Infomercials convince girls they need diet pills.

☐ In some countries, anorexia is related to religious purposes.

2 Which statement can't you find in the text?

1. Eating disorders are spreading. ☐
2. Eating disorders are increasing worldwide. ☐
3. Doctors are responsible for prescribing diet pills. ☐
4. Media plays an import role in the spread of eating disorders. ☐

3 Look at the words taken from the text and choose the best translation.

1. ...that allow <u>speedy</u>, world-wide communication.
   a. veloz ☐
   b. velocidade ☐
   c. rapidamente ☐
2. ...the rise in the <u>rates</u> of eating disorders in European countries...
   a. ratos ☐
   b. porções ☐
   c. porcentagem ☐
3. ...anorexia is not <u>induced</u> by a desire...
   a. ajudada ☐
   b. causada ☐
   c. aumentada ☐
4. Infomercials for <u>weight-losing products</u>...
   a. produtos sem peso ☐
   b. produtos que perdem peso ☐
   c. produtos para perder peso ☐
5. ...and <u>channeling</u> this desire...
   a. direcionando ☐ b. levando ☐ c. canal ☐

Hyperlinks

food + health

LINK 7

LINK 8

LINK 8

LOG IN

1 Do you look at the labels on food items before buying them?

2 How can you use the information on food labels?

WORD BANK

healthy: saudável
label: rótulo, etiqueta
nutrition facts label: tabela nutricional
packages: pacotes, embalagens
serving size: tamanho da porção
serving: porção

NOTES

(25) Nutrition Facts Label

Food labels seem difficult to understand, and many people don't really read them, do they? What information can you get from the food label below? ***Take a good look at it.***

Valeur Nutritionnelle / Nutritional Information		
Valeurs Typiques / Typical Values	Pas/Per biscuit	Pas/Per 100g
Valeur Energétique/ Energy Values	480 KJ	2130 KJ
Valeur Energétique/ Energy Values	115 kcal	510 kcal
Protéines / Protein	1,3g	5,8g
Glucides / Carbohydrate	13,2g	58,7g
dont: sucres / of which sugars	6,5g	29,0g
Lipides / Fat	6,1g	27,1g
dont: saturés / of which saturates	3,4g	15,0g
Fibres / Fibre	0,8g	3,7g
Sodium	0,08g	0,35g
Équivalent en sel / Equivalent of salt	0,20g	0,89g

Was it easy to understand? Do you know how each of the items is intended to help you? Look at the text from the U.S. Food and Drug Administration to find out more.

(26) How to Understand and Use the Nutrition Facts Label

People look at food labels for different reasons. [...] The following label-building skills are intended to make it easier for you to use nutrition labels to make quick, informed food choices that contribute to a healthy diet.

THE NUTRITION FACTS LABEL: AN OVERVIEW

The Serving Size

The first place to start when you look at the Nutrition Facts label is the serving size and the number of servings in the package. Serving sizes are standardized to make it easier to compare similar foods; they are provided in familiar units, such as cups or pieces, followed by the metric amount, e.g., the number of grams.

The size of the serving on the food package influences the number of calories and all the nutrient amounts listed on the top part of the label. **Pay attention to the serving size, especially how many servings there are in the food package. Then ask yourself, "How many servings am I consuming?" (e.g., 1/2 serving, 1 serving, or more)** [...].

Calories (and Calories from Fat)

Calories provide a measure of how much energy you get from a serving of this food. Many Americans consume more calories than they need without meeting recommended intakes for a number of nutrients. The calorie section of the label can help you manage your weight (i.e., gain, lose, or maintain). **Remember: the number of servings you consume determines the number of calories you actually eat (your portion amount).**

[...]

General Guide to Calories

40 Calories is low
100 Calories is moderate
400 Calories or more is high
[...]

The Nutrients: How Much?

[...]

The nutrients listed first are the ones Americans generally eat in adequate amounts, or even too much. [...] Eating too much fat, saturated fat, trans fat, cholesterol, or sodium may increase your risk of certain chronic diseases, like heart disease, some cancers, or high blood pressure.

[...]

Most Americans don't get enough dietary fiber, vitamin A, vitamin C, calcium, and iron in their diets. [...] Eating enough of these nutrients can improve your health and help reduce the risk of some diseases and conditions. [...]

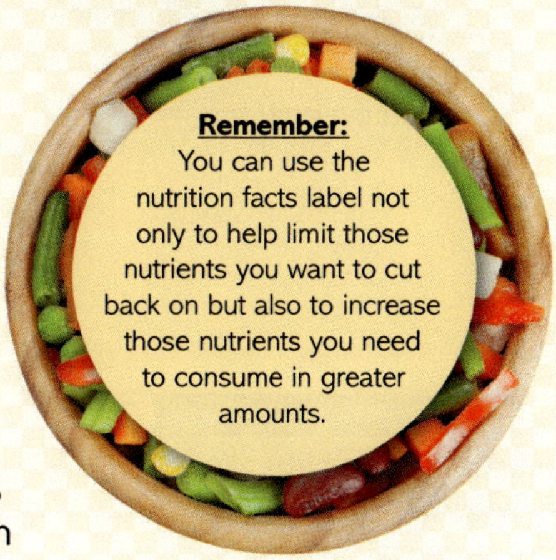

Extracted from: www.fda.gov/Food/ResourcesForYou/Consumers/NFLPM/ucm274593.htm

UNCOVERING THE *TEXT*

TOPIC

____

GENRE

What kind of texts are on pages 86 and 87?

- [ ] table
- [ ] letter
- [ ] novel
- [ ] article

1 **Look at the subtitles. What information can you infer from them?**

____

Examining subtitles is a reading strategy!

Quando examinamos o subtítulo para uma seção, podemos ter uma ideia do tipo de informação que encontraremos naquela parte do texto e voltar nossa atenção para esse tópico.

2 **Read the sentences, find evidence in the text to support or contradict them, then mark T for *true* or F for *false* and write the sentence that made you decide.**

1. People look at the labels only to check the amount of calories. [ ]

____

2. The nutrition facts label offers detailed information. [ ]

____

3. The serving sizes are standard all over the world. [ ]

____

4. The calorie section can help people who are on diets to choose what to buy. [ ]

____

5. The nutrition facts label helps people who want to lose weight. [ ]

____

____

RELATED LINKS

For more information on this Link's topics, please visit:

http://www.foodtechconnect.com/

http://www.healthyeating.org/

3 **Skim the text and answer the following questions in English or Portuguese.**

1. What is the main purpose of the text?

____

____

2. How are the serving sizes standardized?

____

____

3. What sort of nutrients help to have a healthy life?

____

4. Take a look at the number of calories per biscuit in the table on page 86. According to the text, is that a low, moderate, or high amount of calories?

____

FORUM

Would people eat better if they knew exactly what they are consuming? How can we change and have better eating habits as a population in general?

EXPANDING THE *VOCABULARY*

1 Find the antonyms of the following words in the text.

1. slow ____________________ (topic: How to Understand and Use the Nutrition Facts Label)
2. unhealthy ____________________ (topic: How to Understand and Use the Nutrition Facts Label)
3. unfamiliar ____________________ (topic: The Serving Size)
4. fewer ____________________ (topic: Calories (and Calories from Fat))
5. too little ____________________ (topic: The Nutrients: How Much?)
6. decrease ____________________ (topic: The Nutrients: How Much?)
7. low ____________________ (topic: The Nutrients: How Much?)
8. harm ____________________ (topic: The Nutrients: How Much?)

2 Answer the questions by using one of the underlined words in the text.

1. Which of the words is a verb and means "to have something in your mind as a plan"?
____
2. Which of the words means "consumption"? ____________________
3. Which of the words means "as much as necessary"? ____________________
4. Which verb means the same as "use, drink, and eat"? ____________________
5. Which verb means the same as "give or supply"? ____________________
6. Which noun is a synonym of "quantity"? ____________________
7. Which verb means "direct, control, or succeed in doing something difficult"?
____

3 Find three verbs related to weight in the text.

____

4 Skim the text, find the expressions below, and choose the best alternative.

1. "Informed choices" means...
   a. escolhas informais ☐ b. escolhas bem fundamentadas ☐
2. "Meeting recommended intakes" means...
   a. ingerir a quantidade recomendada ☐ b. encontrar a ingestão recomendada ☐
3. "Diseases and conditions" means...
   a. doenças e problemas de saúde ☐
   b. doenças e circunstâncias ☐

5 Circle the prefixes/suffixes and find out the root words.

1. salty
2. selection
3. encourage
4. daily
5. relation
6. disobey
7. passage
8. irrelevant
9. consumption
10. drainage
11. indifferent
12. incompetence
13. observation
14. discourage
15. greasy

Suffixes

O sufixo ***-ion*** (*-ation*, *-ition*) pode ser acrescentado a verbos para formar substantivos que significam "o processo de" ou "o resultado de". Ex.: informat***ion***, *definit**ion***.

O sufixo ***-age*** pode ser acrescentado a verbos para formar substantivos que significam "o ato de" ou "o resultado do ato de". Ex.: *pack**age**, post**age**, marri**age***.

O sufixo ***-y*** geralmente é acrescentado a substantivos para formar adjetivos e significa "que tem a qualidade de" ou "que tem a aparência etc. de". Ex.: *health**y**, oil**y**, greas**y***.

6 Complete these sentences using the words in exercise 2 or words that are related to them.

1. A person who consumes is a ______________.
2. The way to hell is paved with good ______________.
3. A person that provides something to others is a ______________.
4. If you don't know the procedures, you may ask the ______________.

7 Complete the sentences with the words below.

servings label choices amounts standardize

1. Our body can store vast ______________ of fat.
2. The ______________ he made are not compatible with healthy foods.
3. The government needs to ______________ packaging rules.
4. The ______________ are not always very clear and easy to read.
5. The bag contains six ______________ of pretzels.

8 Choose the best alternative to complete the sentences.

1. She is on a diet to ______________ weight.
   a. gain ☐ b. win ☐ c. get ☐
2. The amount of ______________ is lower than what is recommended.
   a. trans fats ☐ b. diseases ☐ c. nutrients ☐
3. For a healthy diet, you need an ______________ amount of several food items.
   a. even ☐ b. adequate ☐ c. average ☐
4. His fiber ______________ is too low.
   a. intake ☐ b. ingestion ☐ c. quantity ☐
5. Scientists have not been able to find the cure for several ______________.
   a. amounts ☐ b. illness ☐ c. diseases ☐

DISCOVERING GRAMMAR

Tag Questions

Food labels seem difficult to understand, and many people don't really read them, *do they?*

Tag Question (ou Question Tag) é uma pergunta curta feita ao final de uma oração com a finalidade de pedir uma confirmação do que foi dito: You like coffee, *don't you?* (Você gosta de café, não gosta?)

A tag question é sempre formada de verbo auxiliar + pronome.

Food labels can help you organize your diet, *can't they?*

Eating healthy foods is very important, *isn't it?*

Ao fazermos uma *tag question*, precisamos prestar atenção a se a oração a qual ela se refere é afirmativa ou negativa, pois:

Oração afirmativa: *tag* negativa — You are tired, *aren't you?*

Oração negativa: *tag* afirmativa — They won't come, *will they?*

Pay attention!

Frases com verbo *to be* e sujeito *I*: *tag question* com *are(n't)*, não *am*. I'm late, *aren't I?*

Frases no imperativo: *tag question* com *will*. Stop talking, *will you?* Don't shout, *will you?*

Se o sentido da frase for negativo mas a estrutura for afirmativa, a *tag question* será afirmativa.

You never cry, *do you?*

Frases iniciadas por *let's*: *tag question* com *shall we*. Let's dance, *shall we?*

1 Check the correct tag questions for the sentences.

1. Marley was here,
   a. wasn't he? ☐ b. was he? ☐
2. Rebecca didn't see him,
   a. didn't she? ☐ b. did she? ☐
3. You were at the airport at 4:00,
   a. weren't you? ☐ b. were you? ☐
4. Jacob was Larissa's friend,
   a. wasn't he? ☐ b. was he? ☐
5. The food isn't fresh,
   a. isn't it? ☐ b. is it? ☐
6. I can't climb the mountain,
   a. can't I? ☐ b. can I? ☐
7. We haven't received our tickets,
   a. haven't we? ☐ b. have we? ☐
8. Maya is going to school,
   a. isn't she? ☐ b. is she? ☐

2 Match the columns.

1. Leah saw the movie yesterday,	☐ could she?
2. You aren't sixteen years old,	☐ have they?
3. She couldn't stay,	☐ were you?
4. You weren't traveling,	☐ didn't she?
5. They haven't worked hard,	☐ are you?

An opinion

1 Read the e-mail published in a newspaper.

27

To: editor@editor.com
From: josh@josh.com
Subject: Food options at school

Dear Editor,

In my opinion, the food options offered at school should be more varied. For one thing, they always offer the same dishes, rice, beans, beef, poultry, or fish, without offering a good choice for vegetarians.

In addition, the beef is not lean, and the fish and chicken are usually fried. If we want to instill healthier habits, the nutritionist in charge should not offer fried stuff. Roasted or grilled is healthier. Also, there should be more variety in terms of cooked and raw vegetables. Finally, I suggest that fresh fruit be included as dessert.

Josh Griswold, New York.

2 Write an e-mail to a newspaper. Express your opinion about advertising diet foods on TV. Use phrases from the box.

LANGUAGE HELP

- In my opinion, …
- For one thing, …
- I believe that…
- For example, …
- I think (that)…
- In addition, …
- I feel (that)…
- Also, …
- One reason that…
- Finally, …

To:
From:
Subject:

Review

1 **Check the correct alternative.**

1. A: Mayans and Aztecs were the first to cultivate cacao, ______________?

   B: Yes, and Spanish conquerors ______________ cocoa beans to Europe.

   a. weren't they / took ☐
   b. don't they / take ☐
   c. didn't they / were taking ☐

2. A: Coffee has its origins in Africa, ______________?

   B: Yes, it does. Around the ninth century, Ethiopian shepherds observed that the goats ______________ more energy after consuming coffee berries.

   a. didn't it / had ☐
   b. doesn't it / had ☐
   c. does it / have ☐

3. Coffee ______________ to Egypt and Yemen and ______________ a passion in Cairo and Mecca.

   a. spread / became ☐
   b. spreaded / becoming ☐
   c. spread / were becoming ☐

4. The peanut ______________ from Brazil or Peru. It ______________ 3,500 years ago or so.

   a. is / was appearing ☐
   b. were / appear ☐
   c. is / appeared ☐

5. When the explorers ______________ to Spain, they ______________ peanuts with them. Traders spread peanuts to Africa and Asia and then to North America.

   a. were returning / bring ☐
   b. return / brought ☐
   c. returned / brought ☐

6. A: Graves of ancient Incas often contain jars filled with peanuts, _______________?

   B: Yes. It _______________ food for the afterlife.

   a. didn't they / were ☐
   b. don't they / was ☐
   c. doesn't it / is ☐

7. When Columbus _______________ in the West Indies, natives _______________ necklaces and headdresses made of popcorn.

   a. arriving / wearing ☐
   b. has arrived / wore ☐
   c. arrived / were wearing ☐

8. Natives throughout the Americas _______________ popcorn beer and popcorn soup.

   a. were made ☐
   b. made ☐
   c. was making ☐

9. Children often like popcorn, _______________?

   a. did they ☐
   b. do they ☐
   c. don't they ☐

2 **Read and listen to the text. Then underline the sentence with the Past Continuous.**

28

In 1620, by the time the Pilgrims arrived at the New World, popcorn was spreading through almost all tribes of South and North America.

The Native Americans used to bring popcorn to many of the meetings with colonists as a goodwill gesture. Legend says that in Massachusetts, they brought popcorn to the first Thanksgiving.

The colonists loved popcorn so much they served it with sugar and cream for breakfast.

The oldest popcorn was discovered in a cave in central New Mexico. It is thought to be about 5,600 years old.

Ancient poppers made of soapstone, pottery and metal have been found in Indian excavation sites.

sources: www.essortment.com/history-popcorn-41743.html and www.jollytime.com/aboutus/history_of_pop_corn

3 **Complete the following sentences about the text using tag questions.**

1. The oldest popcorn probably dates back to 5,600 years ago, ________________?
2. Popcorn was once served as breakfast, ________________?
3. Native Americans introduced popcorn to Pilgrims, ________________?

4 **Read and listen to the text. Classify the underlined words as verb, adjective, or noun. Write the answer next to the corresponding number.**

29

Cocoa, from which chocolate is created, originated in the Amazon at least 4,000 years ago. Etymologists [1]<u>trace</u> the origin of the word "chocolate" to the Aztec word *xocoatl*, a bitter [2]<u>drink</u> brewed from cacao [3]<u>beans</u>.

Both the Mayans and Aztecs believed the cacao bean had [4]<u>divine</u> properties, suitable for use in the most [5]<u>sacred</u> rituals of birth, [6]<u>marriage</u>, and death.

Legends say that the Spanish [7]<u>explorer</u> Hernando Cortés was having a banquet at an Aztec castle with Montezuma Emperor when he first [8]<u>drank</u> xocoatl.

Source: http://www.smithsonianmag.com/arts-culture/brief-history-of-chocolate.html

1. ____________________
2. ____________________
3. ____________________
4. ____________________
5. ____________________
6. ____________________
7. ____________________
8. ____________________

So far, SO GOOD?

1 **Crossword. Find words from links 7 and 8.**

Across

4. opposite of success
7. unit used to measure the amount of energy a particular food can produce (plural)
8. to have a strong wish for something to happen or be true
9. if you are fat, you want to lose
13. what helps plants, animals, or people to grow (plural); it can be found in food
15. the sport of lifting weights

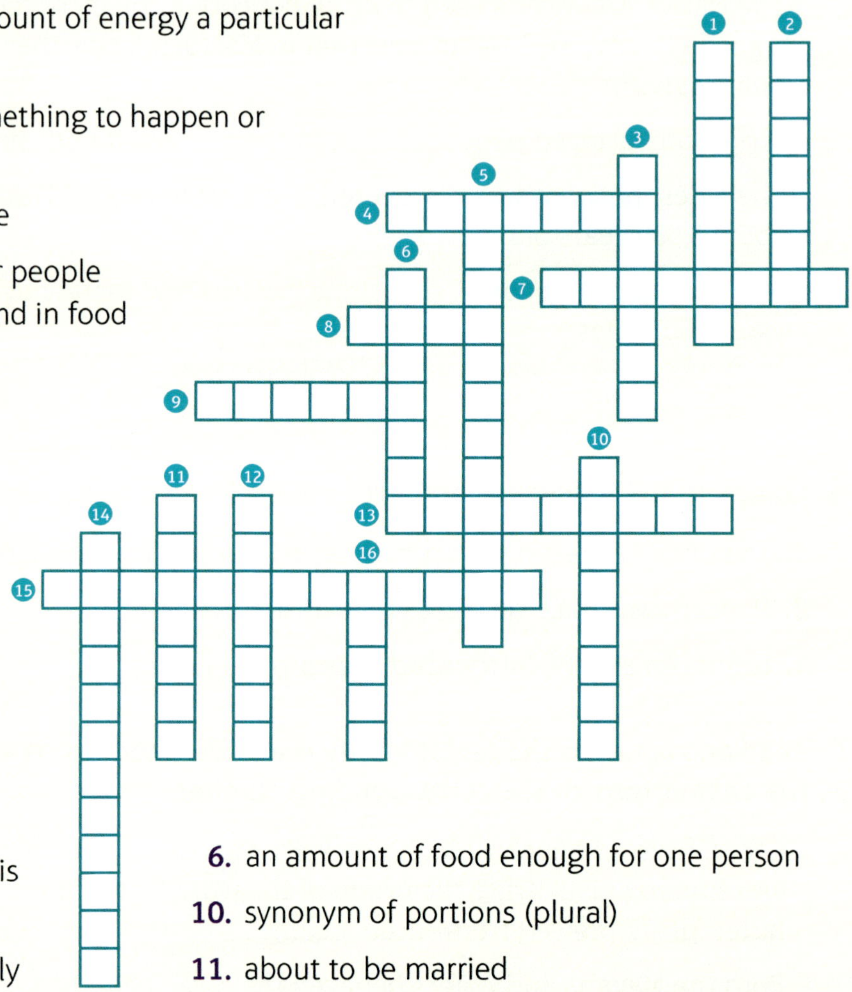

Down

1. the process of getting better after an illness
2. a box, bag, or container food is put in to be sold
3. physically strong and not likely to become sick
5. going across each other
6. an amount of food enough for one person
10. synonym of portions (plural)
11. about to be married
12. the amount of food, drink, etc. that is taken in by someone (plural)
14. the way in which two people behave toward each other
16. the feeling you get when you are afraid (plural)

Now that I've finished links 7 and 8, I can...

...use verbs in the Past Continuous.	☐ Yes!	☐ I still need to study more!
...use tag questions to ask for confirmation.	☐ Yes!	☐ I still need to study more!
...write an e-mail expressing my opinion.	☐ Yes!	☐ I still need to study more!

APPENDICES

UDESC 2012

Read the Text 2 and answer the questions from 36 to 39.

TEXT 2

2012's Second Sun

Earth is believed to be getting a second sun burning in the sky near the end of 2012, as the second biggest star in the universe, Betelgeuse, is dying, which will lead to "multiple days of constant daylight".

Many ancient cultures have speculated about the appearance of a second sun and this event appears to tie in very closely with the December 21 2012 predictions.

Betelgeuse is the second biggest star in the universe and the eighth brightest in the night sky, Scientists have determined that the star is losing mass at a rapid rate, which indicates it will go supernova very soon.

The light emitted from this exploding star will be so bright that it will appear for a few weeks at the end of 2012 as a second sun in the sky. There may be little if no period of darkness or night according to senior lecturer of physics at the University of Southern Queensland, Brad Carter.

Earth will experience "brightness for a brief period of time for a couple of weeks and then over the coming months it begins to fade and then eventually it will be very hard to see at all", explained the Australian scientist Brad Carter to news.com.au.

Scientists have known about this dying star which is 640 light years away from Earth, since 2005. It is believed that as Betelgeuse goes supernova it will not be harmful to Earth. "There will be neutrinos emitted during the supernova process, said University of Minnesota physics professor Priscilla Cushman, but neutrinos, even lots and lots of them, are only weakly interacting, so they won't affect life on earth", but that is only speculation at this point.

The fact is, we as human beings have never experienced anything like this before so close to our home planet, and to be honest, we just don't know for sure what this event could bring.

(www.december212012.com) on 30/08/11

1 **Mark the correct alternative.**

The phrasal verb "tie in" (line 5) means:

a. ☐ to match

b. ☐ to go against to

c. ☐ to determine

d. ☐ to fix

e. ☐ to fasten

2 **The words "biggest" (line 6) and "brightest" (line 6) are examples of:**

a. ☐ inferiority

b. ☐ comparative of superiority

c. ☐ superlative

d. ☐ equality

e. ☐ synonyms

UFAL 2008 ano 1

Danger is Their Middle Name, Thrill-seeking is in Their Genes

The great ones will tell you that when the moment comes there is no fear. But Matt Epper is afraid. He didn't think he would be. Maybe a little, but not like this. Everyone said that it would be easy: his sister, his uncle, even his grandmother.

But as he stands on the edge of the roof looking down at the ground, he can't hear any of them screaming for him to jump. All he can hear is his own heartbeat racing so fast that he feels like his chest might explode.

The boy is 10 years old. His hair is as blond as Southern California. And he has thought about this moment since he was 5 or 6. But now that it's finally here, he isn't so sure anymore. Then, out of the corner of his eye, he sees his mother. "Just jump, Matt! Come on! There's nothing to it! Just kick your legs out and fly!"

What the hell is going on? Why would a mother tell her own son to jump off a roof? What kind of sense does that make?

But it's his mother, so he puts aside his fear, closes his eyes, and jumps. There's a big smile on his face. It's over.

He's safe. And just like that, the 10-year-old boy has become an Epper.

Matt's mother, Eurlyne, is a stuntwoman. His uncles and aunts are stuntpeople too. Even his grandmother is a stuntwoman. And if Matt winds up jumping off roofs for a living when he grows up, he'll take his place in the fourth generation of Eppers in the family business.

Adapted from "Danger is Their Middle Name, Thrill-seeking is in Their Genes", Entertainment Weekly, October 19, 2007, page 92).

3 **The word "stuntpeople", in the last paragraph, refers to people who**

a. Do dangerous acts in a film so that the actors don't have to take risks.

b. Do funny performances in a film so that the audience will laugh.

c. Are the subject of a cinema picture so that they may be famous.

d. Carry the cameras around the studio set so that a film can be made.

e. Write a play or other material to be spoken on radio or TV or in a film.

4 **The phrase "Just jump, Matt! Come on! Just kick your legs out and fly!" expresses**

1) Invitation.
2) Order.
3) Promise.
4) Encouragement.
5) Question.

The correct answers are

a. 2, 3 and 4 only.
b. 1, 2 and 4 only.
c. 1 and 3 only.
d. 3 and 4 only.
e. 1, 2, 3, 4 and 5.

UFT 2012

Read the following poem to answer questions 19 and 20:

Our Conquering Swords

Christopher Marlowe (1564-1593)

1. Our conquering swords shall marshall us the way
2. We use to March upon the slaughter'd foe,
3. Trampling their bowels with our horses' hoofs,
4. Brave horses bred on the white Tartarian hills.
5. My camp is like to Julius Caesar's host,
6. That never fought but had the victory;
7. Nor in Pharsalia was there such hot war
8. As these, my followers willingly would have.
9. Legions of spirits, fleeting in the air,
10. Direct our bullets and our weapons' points,
11. And make your strokes to wound the senseless light;
12. And when she sees our bloody colours spread,
13. Then Victory begins to take her flight,
14. Resting herself upon my milk-white tent--
15. But come, my lords, to weapons let us fall;
16. The field is ours, the Turk, his wife, and all.

Glossary:
Fleeting - passing quickly; lasting only a short time.
Shall - modal verb indicating future predictions.
Slaughter - kill (animals or people) in large numbers.
Sword - weapon with a long thin metal blade and a protected handle.
Trample - tread heavily on sth/sb so as to cause damage or destruction.
Wound - give a wound to (sb). Wound (n): injury caused deliberately to part of the body by cutting, shooting, etc, esp. as the result of an attack.

Available at: www.poetry-archive.com/m/marlowe_christopher.html

5 **The main idea of the poem is:**

a. An agreement of peace between two peoples.
b. An apology to the Muslim Empire.
c. An invitation to soldiers to surrender in the battle of Pharsalia.
d. A prayer to those who bred the brave horses.
e. An encouragement to soldiers going to war.

6 **Mark the CORRECT answer according to the poem:**

a. The words –conquering– (line 1) and –trampling– (line 3) are in the same grammatical category because they are both adverbs.
b. –Our– (line 1) is a possessive pronoun, while –us– (line 1) is a possessive adjective.
c. The pronoun –their– (line 3) refers to the word –swords–.
d. The suffix –less– represents –lack of–, so the word –senseless– (line 11) means without sense.
e. The construction –milk-white– (line 14) is an adverb.

Mackenzie 2012

Go Easy on Yourself

By Stuart Bradford

Do you treat yourself as well as you treat your friends and family?

That simple question is the basis for a new area of psychological research called Self-compassion — how __ (I) __ people view themselves. People who find it __(II)__ to be supportive and understanding to others often score __(III)__ low on self-compassion tests. They get __ (IV) __ with themselves for perceived failures like being overweight or not exercising.

ANXIOUS

The research suggests that accepting our imperfections may be the first step toward better health. People who score high on tests of self-compassion have less depression and anxiety, and tend to be happier and more optimistic. Preliminary data suggest that self-compassion can even influence how much we eat and may help some people lose weight.

This idea does to contrast with the advice of many doctors and self-help books, which suggest that willpower and self-discipline are the keys to better health. But Kristin Neff, a pioneer in the field, says self-compassion is not to be confused with self-indulgence or lower standards.

"I found in my research that the biggest reason people aren't more self-compassionate is that they are afraid they'll become self-indulgent," said Dr. Neff, an associate professor of human development at the University of Texas at Austin. "They believe self-criticism is what keeps them in line. Most people have gotten it wrong because our culture says being hard on yourself is the way to be."

www.nytimes.com

7 **The message conveyed by the text states that**

a. Anxiety and depression can be overcome by reading self-help books.
b. Being hard on yourself is the way to be.
c. self-criticism is immediately linked with self-indulgence.
d. We'd better forgive and love ourselves even if we fail.
e. Willpower is a psychological side of self-compassion if associated with self-criticism and overcoming of personal failures.

8 **The words that properly fill in the blanks I, II, III and IV in the text are:**

a. Kind, easily, surprising and anger.
b. Kind, easily, surprise and angrily.
c. Kindly, easy, surprisingly and angry.
d. Kindly, easily, surprisingly and angrily.
e. Kind, ease, surprising and anger.

ITA 2013

As questões de 14 a 20 referem-se ao texto a seguir:

Reboot the School

SALMAN KHAN'S YOUTUBE LESSONS HAVE ALREADY MADE HIM A GEEK CELEBRITY.

NOW HE WANTS TO REINVENT HOMEWORK, BANISH CLASSROOM LECTURES—AND MAYBE SAVE EDUCATION.

Fifth-graders at Eastside College Preparatory School in East Palo Alto, Calif., sit at their desks with netbooks. They're in the middle of a math lesson, listening as a teacher explains how to convert percentages to decimals. "If we get rid of the percent sign, we just have to move the decimal sign two places to the left," the instructor says. Pens scribble across notebooks.

Eleven thousand miles away in Accra, Ghana, students at the African School for Excellence are studying logarithms. Their teacher is the same one firing off math tips in California–both groups of kids are learning by watching online videos. While the screen shows a march of equations and diagrams, the students never <u>actually</u> see the face of the lecturer. There's just a voice, deep, patient and unrehearsed—think NPR host crossed with Mister Rogers. His inflection rises at times to underscore a point or when he gets really excited. "Math is not just random things to memorize and regurgitate on a test next week," he says. "It's the purest way of describing the universe!"

The voice belongs to Salman Khan, a 35-year-old hedge-fund manager turned YouTube professor to millions around the world. Thanks to his Khan Academy, an online repository of some 3,250 digital lectures, he has become a celebrity to techies, educators and uncounted high schoolers cramming for the AP biology test. His 18-minute discourse on the Krebs cycle and cell metabolism has been viewed more than 675,000 times.

But Khan isn't satisfied with being the most famous teacher ever to appear on a Web browser. He believes he has stumbled onto a solution to some of education's most intractable problems, with his video-driven teaching method at its heart. He wants to fundamentally change the role of teachers in the classroom—and redefine the concept of homework along the way. And he has persuaded Bill Gates, Google's Eric Schmidt and a minor constellation of <u>other tech billionaires to back this quest</u>.

Education reform is notoriously difficult. K-12 schools are debating everything from teacher evaluations to standardized tests, with no consensus in sight. Universities, meanwhile, are confronting massive budget cuts and new kinds of competition—as dramatized by the recent turmoil at the University of Virginia. Its board fired the president amid worries that UVa wasn't keeping up with change and embracing online education fast enough, then rehired her 16 days later after a backlash from students and faculty.

At all levels, there's plenty of skepticism about any tech-centric approach to teaching. An estimated $65.7 billion was spent in the U.S. last year on education technology, according to research firm Gartner. But many educators say there is little concrete proof of its benefits.

Khan is already butting up against veteran teachers nervous about their roles in his brave new classroom. But the biggest obstacle of all may be Khan himself. For all his grassroots fandom and Silicon Valley cred, he's not an educator, and he's never worked with children. Are parents and teachers ready to upend hundreds of years of precedent about how basic subjects are taught on the word of a guy who has spent more time analyzing financial statements than standing before a blackboard?

Fonte: Time, July 9, 2012. Texto adaptado.

9 **A palavra "teaching", em "video-driven teaching method" (linha 19),**

a. ☐ deve ser traduzida por "ensinando".

b. ☐ tem a mesma função gramatical da palavra "YouTube", na construção "YouTube professor" (linhas 12 e 13).

c. ☐ refere-se à palavra "video".

d. ☐ tem a mesma função gramatical da palavra "professor", na construção "YouTube professor" (linhas 12 e 13).

e. ☐ tem a mesma função gramatical da palavra "turned", na construção "turned YouTube professor" (linhas 12 e 13).

10 **Nas frases "Their teacher is the same one firing off math tips in California [...]" (linha 6) e "Its board fired the president amid worries [...]" (linha 26)**

a. ☐ "firing off" e "fired", embora utilizados em tempos verbais diferentes, têm o mesmo significado.

b. ☐ "firing off" equivale a sending quickly.

c. ☐ "firing off" e "fired" têm sentidos opostos.

d. ☐ "firing off" e "fired" podem ser substituídos, respectivamente, por shooting off e shot.

e. ☐ "firing off" equivale a spread e "fired" equivale a detonate.

ANSWER KEY

UDESC 2012

1. A
2. C

UFAL 2008

3. A
4. B

UFT 2012

5. E
6. D

Mackenzie 2012

7. D
8. C

ITA 2013

9. B
10. B

Link 1

1 Give the question for the sentences below. Pay attention to the words in bold when writing the questions.

1. ______________________________?
   Mike is going to join us tomorrow.
2. ______________________________?
   I will spend my vacation **in Paris**.
3. ______________________________?
   Ellen is going downtown **by bus**.
4. ______________________________?
   They will show **the results** next meeting.
5. ______________________________?
   The Hayes will get here **on Monday morning**.
6. ______________________________?
   They are going to bring me **a new camera**.

2 Complete the sentences using the Future Perfect tense or the Future Continuous tense.

1. By the end of this month, Joan ______________ (finish) her final project.
2. Tomorrow, at this exact time, I ______________ (fly) to Germany.
3. They ______________ (examine) the samples on Monday afternoon.
4. Vulk and Thomas ______________ (earn) a lot of money by the end of the year.
5. Are you sure we ______________ (meet) them at 2 o'clock this afternoon?
6. The kids ______________ (learn) enough to do the examinations and get excellent results.
7. I am sure Clair ______________ (send) me an answer before the day ends.

3 Match the columns appropriately.

1. We are planning to go to the beach on Sunday. We think…	[ ] won't be working on that day.
2. If they don't find time to go now…	[ ] they will have to wait for another chance.
3. By the end of the week, we…	[ ] will choose the white jacket or the black one.
4. Louis doesn't know if he…	[ ] we will take some food with us.
5. Tuesday is a holiday. The teachers…	[ ] will have met the coordinator for the meeting.

4 **Read the following text and circle the best alternative for each gap.**

"Frank [1]_______________ to Rio de Janeiro next month. He [2]_______________ at a hotel in Leblon, but doesn't know how much he [3]_______________ on that. Sharon, his girlfriend, [4]_______________ him there because she [5]_______________ a doctor's appointment at the exact time of his flight. They [6]_______________ there for a week, and by the end of the trip, they [7]_______________ many touristic attractions."

1. will going / will go / going to go / is going go / will have gone
2. is going stay / will stays / will be staying / will have stayed / stay
3. will spends / is going spend / is have spent / will spend / is going spending
4. is meeting / will to meet / will meets / is going meet / will has met
5. will has / will to have / has / wills has / will haves
6. are going be / are going to be / will are / going to be / are going to are
7. will seen / will have see / will has see / will have / will have seen

5 **There are many different meanings for the word *will*. Look it up in a dictionary, and then read the sentences and identify the word *will* as *N* for *noun* or *AV* for *auxiliary verb*.**

1. Will ☐ is sick. He will ☐ have to see a doctor against his will ☐ because he hates hospitals.
2. What will ☐ his kids' name be? I am not sure if he will ☐ be called Mark or Will ☐. Do you know what his will ☐ is? To name his kid after that actor, Will ☐ Smith.
3. Willy will ☐ have to read Will's ☐ grandfather's will ☐ because Will will ☐ be too nervous to understand what is written in the will ☐.

6 **Read the sentences below and correct a mistake in each of them.**

1. I believe that by the end of the day everyone will has finished their tasks.

____

2. I'm not complaining about who you going out with tonight!

____

3. They are going choose the best candidate tomorrow morning.

____

4. Do you know if will Jack stay for dinner?

____

Link 2

1 **Fill in the spaces using *somebody*, *nobody*, *anybody*, *something*, *nothing*, or *anything*.**

1. They need ______________ strong enough to carry their luggage.
2. Craig loves ______________ else, except chocolate.
3. We aren't going to buy ______________ from that man. He looks suspicious!
4. Would you like ______________ to drink, Miss Jacks?
5. The priest isn't speaking to ______________ this afternoon. He is sick!
6. ______________ knows the rules. We are new here!

2 **Rewrite the sentences, changing the underlined words without changing the meaning of the sentences.**

1. Carlie isn't meeting <u>anybody</u> tomorrow.
   Carlie is meeting nobody tomorrow.
2. Patricia needs <u>nothing</u> to read before the debate.
   ____
3. We aren't going <u>anywhere</u> this weekend.
   ____
4. I know <u>nobody</u> in the city where I'm going.
   ____
5. Sheila wants to see <u>no one</u> now.
   ____
6. Keith doesn't eat <u>anything</u> at night.
   ____

3 **Choose one of the words in *italics* to complete each sentence.**

1. He can't have everything. He has to choose *nothing / something*!
2. Would you like to *buy something / anything* for your wife?
3. Harry is the best player. *Nobody / Somebody* can win this competition but him.
4. It is necessary to find *nowhere / somewhere* comfortable to spend the night.
5. Gary is inviting *nobody / anybody* to dinner but us.
6. Is there a restaurant *nowhere / anywhere* around?

4 **Complete the sentences with *some*, *any*, *no,* or *none*. There might be more than one possible answer.**

1. The directors are bringing ____________ good news.
2. Is there ____________ option for us to choose?
3. They need ____________ extra staff for the end of the year.
4. The book doesn't bring ____________ text about science. At least, I found ____________.
5. We saw ____________ movies this weekend, but ____________ were about love.
6. They are having a hard time finding good actors. They chose none from the last casting. Would you recommend ____________?

5 **Add an indefinite pronoun to complete each sentence.**

1. Ivan put his glass on the table, but ____________________ moved it!
2. Does ____________________ have change for a dollar so I can buy a sandwich?
3. I was very sad because ____________________ that I called came to my birthday dinner.
4. Noemi was so annoying that ____________________ wanted to sit next to her.
5. ____________________ left the door open!
6. Mom said I could go ____________________ I wanted. I chose Berlin.
7. That painting is so simple. ____________________ could have painted it.
8. ____________________ can bake a cake like Grandma Anna. Hers are the best!

6 **Give answers for the following questions using *nobody* or *no one/nothing/nowhere/none*. Follow the example.**

1 How many e-mails did you answer today?
None

2 Where are you going this weekend?
____

3 Which of these covers do you prefer?
____

4 Who were you talking to in the room?
____

5 How much are you spending this weekend?
____

Link 3

1 Complete the sentences with *must*, *can*, *could*, or *should*, according to the context.

1. We ______________ use the computer at the library yesterday.
2. He ______________ play the guitar and also the piano.
3. ______________ I go to the movies with my friends tonight?
4. The sign says: You ______________ turn off your cell phone. You are at a hospital!
5. It's probably going to rain. You ______________ take an umbrella.
6. I ______________ do my homework today because tomorrow I won't have time.
7. In my opinion, he ______________ see a doctor.
8. They ______________ play musical instruments when they were kids.
9. Visitors ______________ stay here. Only authorized personnel can go into this room.
10. You ______________ not hang around with those people anymore. That's my advice.

2 Rewrite the sentences using *should*, *must*, *mustn't*, or *might*. Remember not to change the meaning of the sentences.

1. I think it is much better if you go home now. You look terrible!

   ____

2. People are prohibited from eating in this meeting room.

   ____

3. I am not allowed to talk about politics here.

   ____

4. We will probably stay home tonight.

   ____

5. The kids have to respect the rules!

   ____

3 Read the following sentences and correct the mistakes in each of them.

1. Danielle ought pay attention to class.

   ____

2. Might they to come later to this session?

   ____

3. They couldn't to play video games before dinner.

___

4. What we can do to help her?

___

5. The director may feels sad with the news.

___

6. Brazil can will become a rich country one day.

___

4 The following rules are from a hotel. Rewrite them using *You must/mustn't*.

1. No washing clothes in the bedroom.

___

2. No receiving guests in the bedroom after 10 P.M.

___

3. Leave your room at 10 A.M. on the last day.

___

4. No smoking in the room.

___

5. Turn off the TV when you leave the room.

___

6. No making noise after midnight.

___

7. No listening to loud music after 8 P.M.

___

5 Complete the gaps with *can, can't, could,* or *couldn't*.

1. You ________ take your driving test until you are 18.
2. We ________ go now. It's stopped raining.
3. We ________ go to the birthday party because we went to a wedding reception.
4. Last week he ________ come to school because he was ill.
5. Not many people ________ run a marathon in less than 3 hours.
6. I ________ swim even when I was a baby.
7. You ________ install this program without a password. It is forbidden!

Link 4

1 **Fill in the spaces using *who, which,* or *whose* where necessary. Write an X in the box if the relative pronoun can be dismissed.**

1. Phil is the boy _______________ has a blue doll. ☐
2. That is the woman _______________ had a car crash last year. ☐
3. I am not buying that CD _______________ cover has a lizard printed on it. ☐
4. Kim is the nurse _______________ I got some help from in the morning. ☐
5. I wish I could meet Bill, _______________ mother is a famous singer. ☐
6. Ron likes food _______________ is made by his granny. ☐
7. The banker is keeping the money _______________ I gave him. ☐

2 **Rewrite the sentences using *who, which,* or *whose.***

1. Michael studies chemistry. He wants to be very famous.

   ____

2. My father loved the book. I gave it as a present.

   ____

3. Have you been to this museum? Its rooms are enormous.

   ____

4. They don't understand this text. It was written by Shakespeare.

   ____

5. Barack Obama is from Hawaii. He was the first African-American president of the USA.

   ____

6. Brazil is very popular among tourists. Brazil is the largest country in South America.

   ____

3 **Read the sentences and circle the only correct alternative for each.**

1. We love that bakery *which / where* delicious donuts and brownies are made.
2. Do you like that market *which / where* fresh fruits and vegetables are sold every day?
3. Robert is going to a club *which / where* is located outside the city.
4. Does Juliet know the restaurant *which / where* Jeff works?
5. I need to go to a place *which / where* people cannot find me!
6. São Paulo is a city *which / where* hosts people from all over the world.

Grammar

4 **Write C if the sentence is correct and I if incorrect. Then, correct the ones in which you find a mistake.**

1. I'm not sure if this is the group of people who you want to meet. ☐

___

2. Tell us if that is the car which she wants to buy. ☐

___

3. Do they know the girl who mother is living abroad? ☐

___

4. Lilian is afraid that she lost the flash drive which contains all the information. ☐

___

5. Are they living in that house where has four bedrooms? ☐

___

6. Polly is watching the movie in which Antonio Banderas pretends to be a man who is a millionaire. ☐

___

5 **Match the sentences.**

1. Rock and roll is a rhythm…	which ☐	…you can find many Buddhist temples. ☐
2. China is a country…	whose ☐	…wasn't very popular in the past. ☐
3. Madonna is someone…	who ☐	…voice and stage performance were unique. ☐
4. Elvis Presley was a singer…	where ☐	…is popular all over the planet! ☐

6 **Complete the sentences below using a Relative Pronoun.**

1. My teacher is a person ___

___

2. English is a language ___

___

3. Brazil is a place ___

___

Link 5

1 Fill in the blanks with the Simple Past of the verbs in the box.

rain – die – kiss – arrive – finish – clean – cook – stay – work

1. The teacher ________________ (neg) late yesterday.
2. She ________________ a very good meal last week.
3. I ________________ my homework the day before yesterday.
4. I ________________ (neg) my room yesterday.
5. They ________________ each other on the weekend.
6. My cat ________________ (neg) last week.
7. Paul ________________ home yesterday.
8. My parents ________________ until eleven o'clock yesterday.
9. It ________________ a lot in Canada three years ago.

2 Complete the mini conversations below using the Simple Past.

1. A: Yesterday ____________ (be) a great day! I ____________ (walk) for one hour before work.

   B: Congratulations! I see you ____________ (exercise) a lot the last few days. That's very important.

   A: Yes. I ____________ (try) very hard to change my habits and I ____________ (manage) to do it.

2. A: Last week I ____________ (work) a lot! It ____________ (be) a very long week, but on the weekend I ____________ (play) video games and ____________ (watch) lots of movies, so today I'm feeling very well.

   B: Great! It's good to rest on the weekend so you can start the week in a good mood!

3. When I ____________ (be) a kid, my mom ____________ (try) to teach me how to play the piano. I ____________ (not/learn) it back then, but I ____________ (want) to try again.

4. A: Last night, when I ____________ (look) at the sky, I ____________ (notice) it was going to rain. I ____________ (need) an umbrella to go home, but I ____________ (not/have) one with me. Then, you ____________ (show up) with an extra one! That ____________ (be) a miracle!

   B: Well, you ____________ (be) lucky yesterday. Next time, take an umbrella with you!

5. A: ____________ you ____________ (watch) the movie on TV yesterday?

   B: Not really. I ____________ (be) very tired and ____________ (decide) to go to bed early.

   A: Well, I ____________ (watch) it.

3 Read the following paragraph and make questions that fit the answers below.

When I was 12 years old, I moved to a new house. My old house was very nice. I visited it yesterday, and it is very different now. When I was 12, I played basketball in the backyard; my mom cooked in the kitchen and talked to me at the same time because there was a window from where she could see me playing. My dad studied a lot because he wanted to get a graduate degree in geology. My brother and I liked to play video games together. My sister watched TV for a long time, but also helped my mom in the kitchen. I helped too, and I learned many recipes by watching my mom cook. My brother and I cleaned the house on weekends. I also needed to keep my room tidy, or else my mother would really tell me off. At night, we used to fall asleep on the sofa and our father carried us to the bedroom. That was very nice, but it's good that things are different now, too.

1. ______________________________?

He was 12 years old when he moved to the new house.

2. ______________________________?

He visited the old house yesterday.

3. ______________________________?

He talked about the old house.

4. ______________________________?

He played basketball when he was 12.

5. ______________________________?

His mom cooked while he played basketball.

6. ______________________________?

His father studied a lot because he wanted a graduate degree.

7. ______________________________?

No, his sister didn't play video games with them.

8. ______________________________?

He learned recipes watching his mother cook.

9. ______________________________?

They cleaned the house on weekends.

10. ______________________________?

Yes, he liked to see things are different now.

Link 6

1 **Find the past form of the verbs below in the wordsearch.**

throw – bring – eat – buy – catch – go – cut – fly – hit – lose

D	D	T	L	G	W	T	R	A	M	V	C	C	K	T	K	A	T	L	L
D	U	O	R	F	H	W	C	K	F	R	A	H	D	K	H	C	H	Y	L
C	S	B	K	G	Q	A	E	R	U	U	S	L	K	S	X	F	R	G	Y
T	J	S	U	A	V	G	U	L	F	R	A	V	D	T	C	V	E	V	Y
G	J	O	J	G	T	V	G	W	F	H	F	L	K	L	T	B	W	F	J
C	R	Y	G	Q	O	U	W	K	W	M	D	S	U	M	H	G	H	O	I
B	E	G	Y	A	E	N	I	T	O	V	B	V	V	S	R	I	J	F	E
H	T	S	B	I	W	R	B	V	D	W	T	C	O	I	I	R	E	O	Q
Y	A	V	P	V	T	Q	Q	R	R	U	P	R	F	Q	C	G	J	U	U
X	Q	V	Q	Z	V	W	Q	R	R	T	Z	Z	E	G	Y	F	N	M	O
N	G	V	I	H	I	T	X	J	Y	Z	H	D	V	X	A	V	P	L	G
T	A	C	A	U	G	H	T	B	R	E	Q	U	H	V	F	N	Y	U	B
K	N	N	N	Z	Z	P	G	E	O	G	M	T	M	L	F	B	K	G	W
Y	O	V	N	E	H	L	K	F	D	U	B	H	Y	K	K	A	Q	U	Z
O	P	L	U	B	K	G	T	G	Z	K	G	Y	B	O	Z	M	O	Z	H
J	B	I	S	R	O	W	P	D	G	V	T	H	R	P	A	S	N	I	H
S	G	X	I	N	K	D	U	W	C	A	R	V	T	X	A	S	F	I	M
X	P	M	E	L	N	M	D	A	I	O	M	K	K	T	N	E	W	Z	Q

2 **Give the questions to the following answers.**

1. ____?

They spent the night at a hotel.

2. ____?

Aron wrote a message on the board.

3. ____?

The Smiths drove to the beach last weekend.

4. ____?

I got Michael's book.

5. ____?

The kids went to the park by subway.

6. ____?

Jason fell on the floor because he stepped on a banana peel!

3 **Underline and correct the mistakes you find in each sentence.**

1. Who do you speak to last night?

____

2. Who did drive to the coast last holiday?

____

3. What made you went home alone?

____

4. Why did that man hits the wall?

____

5. Did you know Sarah did have all the answers?

____

6. What did you did last night?

____

4 **First, unscramble the letters to find a verb. Then, use the past form of these verbs in sentences about your life.**

1. MECO: ______________

____

2. INW: ______________

____

3. KETA: ______________

____

4. AEWK: ______________

____

5. DENS: ______________

____

6. LETL: ______________

____

7. SOLE: ______________

____

____

8. DSENP: ______________

____

____

Link 7

1 Complete the sentence appropriately.

"I guess while my grandma ______________ TV and my grandpa ______________ his favorite book, my other cousins ______________ with one another around the house."

1. watching / was read / were play ☐
2. was watched / was read / were playing ☐
3. watched / read / was playing ☐
4. was watching / reading / was playing ☐
5. was watching / was reading / were playing ☐

2 Read the sentences and then choose the correct alternatives.

1. What ______________ yesterday at 7?

   a. you did ☐
   b. did you did ☐
   c. was you doing ☐
   d. were you doing ☐
   e. did you doing ☐

2. I ______________ a soccer game on TV when my cell phone rang.

   a. watched ☐
   b. did watch ☐
   c. was watching ☐
   d. were watching ☐
   e. did watching ☐

3. ______________ anything suspicious?

   a. You heard ☐
   b. Did you hear ☐
   c. Did you heard ☐
   d. Was you hearing ☐
   e. Were you hearing ☐

4. Yes, at about seven o'clock, two people ______________ in the hall.

   a. fought ☐
   b. fight ☐
   c. was fighting ☐
   d. were fighting ☐
   e. were fought ☐

5. But I was so interested in the game that I ______________.

   a. pay attention ☐
   b. didn't pay attention ☐
   c. was paying attention ☐
   d. were pay attention ☐
   e. did paying attention ☐

3 **Make four questions for the sentence below.**

"Avril was painting the kitchen while Noam was cooking potatoes."

1. ____?
2. ____?
3. ____?
4. ____?

4 **Read the sentences below, analyze the words in bold, and write *A* for *adjective*, *N* for *noun*, and *V* for *verb*.**

1. **Spelling** [ ] is not a strong feature of her **writing** [ ].
2. Were you **reading** [ ] that **amazing** [ ] story about **competing** [ ] in the Olympics?
3. The **building** [ ] was **being** [ ] rebuilt with governmental financial support.
4. **Coming** [ ] to school by bus in the **morning** [ ] was **driving** [ ] me crazy.
5. **Traveling** [ ] to Paris during the winter improved our **speaking** [ ] in French.

5 **Complete the sentences correctly using the verbs in the box.**

speak – play – meet – start – go – drive – happen – study – wear – do – phone – take

1. Helen ______________ a beautiful dress when I ______________ to her at the party.
2. What ______________ you ______________ when the accident ______________?
3. They ______________ their new truck along a road when it ______________ to rain.
4. Where ______________ he ______________ when I ______________ him on the street?
5. While I ______________ for the test, my sisters ______________ with some dolls at the park.
6. When Trisha ______________ me, I ______________ a shower.

6 **Answer the following questions.**

1. What were you doing yesterday at 7 P.M.?

____

2. Do you think your teacher was working last Friday night?

____

3. Was it raining last weekend?

____

Link 8

1 **Match the columns.**

1. Frank and George hit the ball,
2. The neighbor chose the yellow fence,
3. Tell me the truth,
4. Men don't like to gossip,
5. Ian wasn't paying attention,

☐ will you?
☐ was he?
☐ didn't she?
☐ didn't they?
☐ do they?

2 **Check (✓) the correct sentences. If the sentence is incorrect, put an *X* and correct it.**

1. People hate being criticized, doesn't he? ☐

____

2. Everybody needs attention, don't they? ☐

____

3. Don't show it to the kids, do you? ☐

____

4. Bobby puts the words in order easily, doesn't he? ☐

____

5. No one is coming late today, is he? ☐

____

3 **Give the tag questions for the sentences below.**

1. I'm trying to give my best, _______________?
2. Suzy joined the Army when she was 18 years old, _______________?
3. The computer is no longer working, _______________?
4. Theo spoke to no one about the project, _______________?
5. American singers tend to sing very well, _______________?
6. You'd never understand what I am saying, _______________?
7. Typing fast requires lots of practice, _______________?
8. I am drinking nothing while I eat, _______________?

4 **Circle the correct tag questions for the sentences.**

1. John had dinner here, *didn't he? / did he?*
2. Ron is meeting nobody now, *is he? / isn't he?*
3. Nobody agrees with me, *do they? / don't they?*
4. I am very proud of her grades, *aren't I? / am I?*
5. Sleeping 8 hours is very common, *is it? / isn't it?*
6. Make it work, *will you? / won't you?*
7. The Internet was the greatest invention, *was it? / wasn't it?*
8. My students got great results, *did they? / didn't they?*

5 **Complete the conversation below using tag questions.**

A: Hey, you are that guy from TV, ______________?

B: Yes, that's me. And you're probably a fan, ______________?

A: Actually, your show is not really that good, ______________? I really liked some of your previous work, but it seems to me this one is just for money, ______________?

B: Well, do you want an autograph, a photo, or anything else? You know I'm busy, ______________?

A: I'm sorry. I didn't offend you with my comment, ______________? It was not my intention.

B: No, it's OK. But I really have to go.

A: I'm sorry! Can I just take a picture with you for my children?

B: OK! That's funny, the show was first thought for adults, but kids really like it, ______________? Well, let's take the picture and I'll go.

A: Thank you! It was great meeting you!

B: See you around.

LINK 1 Linked Skills

And I'm back with the weather forecast for the week. We're now going to look at some European cities. Let's start with London: it's a bit chilly, and temperatures won't get higher than 18°C. Have your umbrella with you, as it might rain in the afternoon. In Barcelona though, the sun is shining bright, and people will have a nice time on the beach as the temperature today can reach 26°C. If you're in Paris, you can go for a nice walk without worrying about the weather. The sun won't come out, but the temperature will be around 21°C. It'll also be nice in Berlin, where it'll be 23°C.

LINK 3 Linked Skills

1. Love is the art of making exceptions.
2. Love is incompatible with fear.
3. If you respect others, they will respect you.
4. Good actions are nourishments for youths much more than words.
5. Love is blind; friendship closes its eyes.
6. The old should be treated with respect.

LINK 5 Communication Bytes

Jeff: Hi, Ron! Where were you last weekend?

Ron: At home. Why? What happened?

Jeff: Nothing special. I just wanted to talk to you.

Ron: Why didn't you call me?

Jeff: I did, but your phone was off.

Ron: Oh! That's right. I was tired and decided to switch it off. Sorry.

Jeff: No problem. What did you do?

Ron: I stayed home and relaxed. And you?

Jeff: My weekend was pretty busy.

Ron: Really? Tell me about it.

Jeff: Well, to begin with I didn't stay at home. I went to a great exposition about the Middle Ages and saw incredible inventions. I wanted to invite you to come with me.

Ron: What a pity! I would have loved that! The Middle Ages is one of my favorite history topics.

Jeff: Well, I hope you learned a lesson. Don't switch off your cell phone.

Ron: You're absolutely right.

LINK 5 Linked Skills

What would women do without a mirror? Did you know it was invented by the Sumerians and Egyptians in 3000 B.C.? The toilet was invented in Egypt around 2100 before Christ, but toilet paper was only invented in 1857 by Joseph Gayetty. The wheel is much more recent than the toilet paper, only 5000 years ago in Asia. Although the first modern cars powered by an internal combustion engine were available in 1806, developed by François de Rivaz, the windscreen wipers were invented almost one hundred years later in 1903 by a woman called Mary Anderson. What about the remote control and GPS? The remote control was invented in 1955 by Eugene Polley and the GPS or Global Positioning System has been around for about 50 years. The principal inventor and designer is Roger L. Easton.

LINK 7 Communication Bytes

M: I was thinking of going on a diet.

A: Really? Why?

M: I am a bit overweight, so I read about a "detox diet" and wanted to try it. We live such a stressful life! Detoxing sounds good.

A: Well, it sure does sound good. But how much do you really know about it?

M: It's an all-positive diet! Firstly, you lose weight and in addition to that you detox. They say you gain more energy and feel much better after this process.

A: Unfortunately, that's not completely true. Many doctors have talked about downsides to this kind of diet.

M: Really? What could possibly be bad about this?

A: On the one hand, you may lose weight fast; but on the other hand, you may not get enough nutrients.

M: In short, I may lose weight but not stay healthy, right?

A: Exactly! You should see a doctor before going on a diet. And to be honest, you're not overweight at all!

LINK 7 Linked Skills

I – Interviewer

T – Tiffany

I: Good morning everyone. This is your favorite radio station with the most important news of the moment. A poll on organic food has just been released, and we're here with Tiffany, responsible for an article in *Urban Farm* magazine about the results of the poll. Hi Tiffany, how are you?

T: I'm fine, thanks.

I: So, what can you tell us about the poll?

T: Approximately 3,000 Americans participated in the poll each month, from April 2010 until June 2011. The results were divided into some categories and one of them is the age group. We have three age groups: people who are less than 35 years old; people between 35 and 64; and people who are 65 or older. The results were really interesting.

I: Can you share some of them with us?

T: Of course. For example, when asked if they would prefer to eat organic or non-organic foods, given this choice, most people, in all age groups, said they'd prefer organic foods. Actually, about 63% of people who are less than 35 years old said so. That's a big number! Most people from all ages prefer organic foods not because of the taste, but because they want to support local farmers.

I: That's very interesting. We've just received a tweet with a question for you from one of our listeners, @johnmckee. He asks why people say they prefer organic food but end up buying non-organic.

T: Well, that's also in the poll. People prefer buying non-organic foods because they are cheaper!

I: And that's something we can't deny. Thank you very much, Tiffany.

T: Anytime!

Glossary

A

a - um, uma
ability - capacidade, habilidade
accountability - responsabilidade
achievements - realizações
acronym - acrônimo, iniciais, abreviatura
administration - administração
admit - admitir
adrenalin - adrenalina
advance - avançar
advanced - avançado
adversity - adversidade
advertising - publicidade
advice - conselho
afloat - flutuando
after - depois
age group - faixa etária
aid - auxiliar, ajudar
albacore - atum branco
alleviate - aliviar
allow - permitir
almost - quase
amount - quantidade
angry - zangado(a), com raiva
anybody - alguém
anything - qualquer coisa, nada
anywhere - em qualquer lugar
apparatus - aparelho
appreciate - apreciar
approval - aprovação
archipelago - arquipélago
argue - argumentar, discutir
article - artigo
ass - burro (animal)
astounding - assombroso
astronomer - astrônomo
at all - absolutamente
at least - pelo menos
attend - assistir, comparecer
attire - vestuário
automobile - automóvel
available - disponível
avoid - evitar
award - prêmio
awareness - consciência de algo

B

bad - ruim
banquet - banquete
barracuda - barracuda (tipo de peixe carnívoro)
basket - cesta
beans - feijões
bear - suportar
beauty - beleza
beef - carne
beginners - iniciantes
bell - guizo, sino
belong - pertencer
below - abaixo
beryl - berilo
betterment - aperfeiçoamento
beverage - bebida
beyond - além de
birth - nascimento
biscuits - biscoitos
bitter - amargo
bladder - bexiga (parte do corpo)
blame - culpar, culpa
blind - cego
boundaries - limites
box - caixa
breakfast - café da manhã
breast - peito
breathing - respiração
breeches - calções, calças apertadas que terminam logo abaixo dos joelhos.
brewed - fabricado, bebida preparada com infusão de água quente (chá ou café, por exemplo)
bridge - ponte
bright - brilhante
buckle - fivela
buffoon - bufão
build trust - criar confiança
built up - construiu-se
built - construído
bytes - bytes (informática)

C

cabbage - repolho
cacao - cacau, cacaueiro
cake - bolo
calcium - cálcio
calf - panturrilha
camouflage pattern - padrão de camuflagem (tecidos)
campus - terreno de uma escola
car - carro
carbon - carbono
carbon-free - livre de carbono
career - carreira
caring - cuidadoso(a)
carrot - cenoura
carved - esculpido
cash - dinheiro
castle - castelo
casualties - baixas, mortes
categories - categorias
cave - caverna
century - século
CEO - abreviação de "Chief Executive Officer" (presidente executivo de uma empresa)
certain - determinado, certo
chain - cadeia, corrente
challenge - desafio
character - caráter, personagem
charmed - encantado
charter - contrato, alvará
chasing - perseguição
chicken fillet - filé de frango
chief centers - principais centros
child - criança
childhood - infância
chomp - mastigar ruidosamente
chronic diseases - doenças crônicas
city - cidade
classroom - sala de aula
clothes - roupas
clown - palhaço
coat - casaco
cocoa beans - grãos de cacau
coeducational - escola mista, meninos e meninas estudam juntos

coffee berries - frutos do café
coin - moeda
collapse - queda
commitment - compromisso
community - comunidade
company - empresa, corporação
congestion - congestionamento (trânsito), congestão (nasal, por exemplo)
conquerors - conquistadores
consumption - consumo
content - conteúdo
control - controlar, controle
coral reef - recife de coral
core competencies - competências essenciais
core - centro
cost - custo, custar
costume - traje, figurino, fantasia
cotton - algodão
countryside - campo, interior
courtyard - pátio
cover - cobrir, capa
cowl - capota, capuz
cream sauce - molho cremoso
crest - brasão, crista
crew - tripulação
crispy - crocante
crucial - crucial
culmination - culminação, cume
cup - copo, xícara, taça
curse - amaldiçoar, maldição
cursed - amaldiçoada(o)
cut across - cortar caminho
cut back - cortar, reduzir
cut - cortar, corte

D

damage - danificar, dano
dangled - pendente
data - informação
database - banco de dados
day off - dia de folga
dealership - concessionária
death - morte
decision-making - tomada de decisão
defiantly - desafiadoramente
degree-granting - que concede grau ou título
delectable - deleitável, deliciosa(o)
demand - demanda
deny - negar
desire - desejo
dessert - sobremesa
detox - desintoxicar, desintoxicação
device - dispositivo, aparelho
devil - diabo
dietary fiber - fibra dietética
difficulties - dificuldades
diminish - diminuir
director - diretor
discourage - desencorajar
discovery - descoberta
discriminate - discriminar
disease - doença
dishes - pratos
disobey - desobedecer
display - expor, exposição
disseminate - disseminar
disseminating - divulgação
distaff - fuso de fiar
diver - mergulhador
diving suit - roupa de mergulho
doom - condenar
doomed - condenado
door - porta
doorbell - campainha
downsides - pontos negativos
drainage - drenagem
dress - vestir, vestido

E

e.g. - por exemplo (do latim, exempli gratia)
Earth - planeta Terra
ease - facilidade, facilitar
eating disorder - transtorno alimentar
eccentric - excêntrico
effort - esforço
embarrassment - constrangimento
embody - encarnar
emperor - imperador
employed - empregado(a), utilizado(a)
empower - passar autoridade à alguém
empty - vazio
encompass - envolver
encouraging - animador
endowed - dotado
engaged - (estar) noivo(a)
engine - motor
enough - suficiente
entertain - entreter
entire - todo, completo, total
entry - entrada
equipment - equipamento
especially - especialmente
etymologist - etimologista
eventually - eventualmente
everybody - todo o mundo
everything - tudo
everywhere - em toda parte
experience - experiência
exploration - exploração
explore - explorar
exposed - exposto
extended - alargado
eyeglasses - óculos

F

face - face, rosto, enfrentar
fail - falhar
failure - falha, fracasso
fair - feira
fall asleep - adormecer
falsely - falsamente
far - longe, distante
farsightedness - hipermetropia
fat - gordura
fear - medo, temer
fears - medos
feature - destacar, uma atração ou característica específica de um lugar ou equipamento
feel like - a fim de, com vontade de
finally - finalmente
find - encontrar

fine - multa
first - primeiro
firstly - em primeiro lugar
fish fillet - filé de peixe
float - flutuar
flow - fluxo
flowers - flores
foldable - dobrável
follow - seguir
followed by - seguido de
fool - enganar, tolo
found - encontrado
foundation - fundação
foundered - naufragado
founding - fundador
fox - raposa
frame - quadro, armação de óculos, moldura
free - livre
freedom - liberdade
fresh - fresco
fridge - geladeira
fried chicken - frango frito
fried stuff - frituras
fried - frito
friends - amigos
frown upon - desaprovar
frown - franzir as sobrancelhas

G

gain - ganhar
gale - vento forte
garment - vestuário
gaudy - berrante (cores, roupas)
gesture - gesto
ghosts - fantasmas
girlfriend - namorada
glass - vidro
goat - cabra
goodwill - boa vontade
gooey - macio e grudento
grant - conceder
greasy - gorduroso, oleoso
green beans - vagens
grilled - grelhado
group - grupo
grow up - crescer
guiding - guia, guiando
guild - grêmio

H

hard - difícil, duro
headache - dor de cabeça
headdresses - cocares
healthy - saudável
heart disease - doença cardíaca
height - altura
high blood pressure - pressão alta
high school - colégio
high - alto
hollow reed - haste oca
home - casa, lar
homeless - sem casa
hope - esperança
household - todas as pessoas que moram na mesma casa
however - contudo
hugging - abraçando
human rights - direitos humanos
humankind - humanidade

I

i.e. - ou seja, isto é (do latim, id est)
ice floe - grande bloco de gelo
identity - identidade
in a heartbeat - num piscar de olhos
in addition - além disso, somando-se
in comparison - em comparação
in conclusion - concluindo
in short - resumindo
in - dentro de
industrialized - industrializado
inevitably - inevitavelmente
influence - influenciar
infomercials - comercial com formato de programa de TV
informed - informado
inhaler - inalador
inside - dentro
instill - instilar, gradualmente fazer uma pessoa sentir, pensar ou agir de alguma maneira
intakes - ingestões
interdisciplinary - interdisciplinar
intersecting - interseção, cruzados
intervention - intervenção
invincible - invencível
iron - ferro
island - ilha

J

jack - xaréu (espécie de peixe)
jester - bobo
jibe - piada de mal gosto
job - trabalho
jongleurs - malabaristas
judgement - julgamento
July - julho

K

kayak - caiaque
keep - manter
key factor - fator-chave
kids - crianças
killed - assassinado
know - conhecer, saber
knowledge - conhecimento

L

label - rótulo, etiqueta
lacrosse - jogo de bola com raquetes e duas equipes de 10 jogadores
largest - (o)a maior
late - tarde
laughter - riso
law - lei
lawsuit - ação judicial, processo
lead - levar, liderar
leadership - liderança
league - liga
leave - deixar
legend - lenda

Glossary

length - comprimento
less - menos
let - deixar, permitir
lettuce - alface
library - biblioteca
life - vida
like - como, gostar
limited - limitado
linchpin - mais importante
link - ligação, vínculo
liveliness - vivacidade
lobster - lagosta
local farmers - agricultores locais
long - longo
longer - mais longo, mais tempo
look - olhar
loom - tear
lose - perder
loudly - em volume alto
low-cost - baixo custo
lower - baixar
lunch - almoço

M

magazine - revista
magnifying lenses - lentes de aumento
maintain - manter
manage - gerir
managerial - gerencial
mankind - humanidade
marine park - parque marinho
market share - fatia de mercado
market - mercado
marriage - casamento
mass transit - transporte coletivo
mayor - prefeito
meals - refeições
measure - medir
mentality - mentalidade
merchantman - navio mercante, cargueiro
metric - métrico
Middle Ages - idade Média
mistake - erro
mitigate - mitigar
mock - zombar
modern - moderno
moist - úmido
money - dinheiro
monk - monge
month - mês
motley - manta de retalhos, grupo composto de pessoas ou coisas que não parecem pertencer juntas.
movie producer - produtor de cinema

N

nation - nação
nature - natureza
nearsightedness - miopia
necklace - colar
neighbor - vizinho
network - rede
new - novo, nova
newspaper - jornal
next - próximo
no chance - sem chance
no longer - não mais
nobleman - nobre
nobody - ninguém
nod - assentir
nothing - nada
now - agora
nowadays - hoje em dia
nowhere - lugar nenhum
nudity - nudez
numerous - numeroso
nutrition facts label - tabela nutricional

O

observance - observância
occur - acontecer
old - velho
on the contrary - pelo contrário
on the one hand - por um lado
on the other hand - por outro lado
organic food - alimentos orgânicos
outreach - alcance
outside - do lado de fora
over - sobre, acima
overcome - superar
overnight - durante a noite, que dura uma noite
overtake - ultrapassar
over-the-counter - medicação sem prescrição médica
overview - visão global
overweight - excesso de peso

P

pack - empacotar
packages - pacotes, embalagens
paid - pago
paintings - pinturas
partner - parceiro
party - festa
passion - paixão
peanuts - amendoins
pelagic - pelágico
people - pessoas
perform - representar
performance - atuação
perhaps - talvez
personal - pessoal
persons - pessoas (uso formal)
perspective - perspectiva
phenomenon - fenômenos
pieces - peças
pigeon - pombo
Pilgrims - peregrinos
pill - pílula
pinnacle - pináculo, torre
place - lugar
plague - praga
play - brincar, jogar, tocar, peça
plywood - madeira compensada
poll - pesquisa de opinião
pollution - poluição
popcorn - pipoca
port - porta (informática), cidade portuária onde se carregam e descarregam bens
portrait - quadro, retrato
possible - possível
pottery - cerâmica

poultry - carne de aves, aves criadas para o consumo de sua carne
poverty - pobreza
power - poder
power-driven - movido a motor
prayers - orações
precept - preceito
prediction - previsão
presses - prensas
previously - anteriormente
principal - diretor de escola
printing press - prensa de impressão
private - privado
prolific - prolífico
protection - proteção
provide - fornecer
purpose - propósito

Q

quick - rápido
quite - bastante

R

racism - racismo
rack - prateleira
raise - educar, aumentar o nível de algo
range - alcance
rapidly - rapidamente
rates - taxas
raw - cru
reach - alcançar
reason - razão
received - recebido
records - recordes, registros
recovery - recuperação
reef - recife
regarded - considerado
rejuvenated - rejuvenescido
relationships - relações
released - liberado
relevant - relevante
remain - permanecer
rent - alugar, aluguel
rental car - carro de aluguel
replace - substituir
research - pesquisa
return - voltar
review - rever, revisão
revolutionize - revolucionar
rice - arroz
ride - montar, passeio, carona
rigging - cordame
right - direito
rigorous - rigoroso
rise - subir
road - estrada
roast potato - batata assada
roasted - assado
robber - ladrão
role - papel, função

S

sacred - sagrado
sail - velejar
salty - salgado
same - mesmo, mesma
sand - areia
saturated fat - gordura saturada
scan - examinar, procurar
scholarship - conhecimento, aprendizado
scuba diving - mergulho
seafront - beira-mar
seatbelts - cintos de segurança
secondly - em segundo lugar
see - ver
seemingly - aparentemente
self-contained - autônomo
self-esteem - autoestima
serving size - tamanho da porção
serving - porção
shadow - sombra
shaky - trêmulo (a)
shared - compartilhado
shaved - raspada(o)
sheets - folhas
shepherds - pastores de ovelhas
shipwreck - naufrágio
shocking - chocante
shone - brilhava
shopping cart - carrinho de compras
shortage - escassez
shoulders - ombros
shout - gritar
shroud - mortalha,algo que esconde, cobre
sighting - avistamento
silent - silencioso
single - único
sink - afundar
sinus - cavidades nos ossos do crânio conectadas ao interior do nariz
size - tamanho
skeptical - cético
skidded - derrapou
skill - habilidade
skins - peles
slated - programado
smart - inteligente
smothered - sufocada (o)
soapstone - pedra-sabão
sodium - sódio
solve - resolver
some - algum, alguma, alguns, algumas
somebody - alguém
something - algo
somewhere - em algum lugar
son - filho
space - espaço
spectacles makers - fabricantes de óculos
speech - discurso
speedy - rápido
spindle - eixo
spinning wheel - roda de fiar
split - divisão, dividir
spread - espalhar
stackable - empilhável
staff - equipe de funcionários
stagnant - estagnado
standardized - padronizada(o)
start - começar
state affairs - assuntos de estado
stay - ficar, permanecer
staying - resistente
steam - vapor

Glossary

steamed - cozido (no vapor)
steering wheel - volante
step - passo
stick - vara
sticks - tacos
stiff - duro
still - ainda
stimulation - estimulação
store - armazenar
straight - ininterruptamente, em linha reta
strand - cordão
strategy - estratégia
struggle - lutar, luta
stubborn - teimoso (a)
substance abuse - abuso de substâncias
subtly - sutilmente
such as - tal como
suitable - adequado
sunbathing - banho de sol
support - apoiar, apoio
surgeon - cirurgião
switch off - desligar

T

tail - cauda
take - tomar, pegar, levar
tea - chá
team - equipe
teamwork - trabalho em equipe
tear - rasgar
then - antes
thin - fino
things - coisas
throw - atirar, arremessar
thus - assim
ticking - que produz som de tique-taque
tidy - arrumado
tight - apertado
time bomb - bomba-relógio
tired - cansado
tires - pneus
together - juntos
towards - para, em direção a
traders - comerciantes
trans fat - gordura trans
transportation hubs - centros de transporte
treatment - tratamento
triggered - desencadeada(o)
truly - verdadeiramente
truth - verdade
truthful - verdadeiro
tumbling down - desmoronando
tuna - atum
turn out - acontecer, resultar
twisted - retorcido

U

ubiquitous - onipresente
uncanny - estranho
uncover - descobrir
understand - entender
understanding - compreensão, compreensivo (a)
underwater - subaquático
underwear - roupa íntima
unharmed - ileso
unpack - desempacotar
unrealistic - irrealista
untidy - desordenado
unveil - desvendar
upright - vertical
usually - frequentemente, geralmente

V

values - valores
vanished - desaparecido
vehicle - veículo
veils - véus
vessel - navio
viewers - espectadores
volcanic - vulcânico

W

wait - esperar
walls - paredes
wander away - vagar
warm - quente
watch - ver
waters - águas
wave - onda, acenar
wedding - casamento
week - semana
weight - peso
weightlifting - levantamento de pesos
weight-losing - perda de peso
well-paid - bem pago
western - ocidental
What a pity! - que pena!
wheel - roda
who else - quem mais
whose - cujo(a)
wine-and-olive press - prensa de uvas e azeitonas
wire - arame, fio
wisely - sabiamente
without - sem
woman - mulher
wool - lã
world - mundo
world-class - de classe mundial
world-wide - mundial
worth - valor
wound - ferida
wreck - naufrágio
writing - escrita
wrong - errado

Y

yarn - linha para tricotar, fio
yet - ainda assim, ainda
youth - juventude

Irregular Verbs

Infinitive	Simple Past	Past Participle	Translation
be	was / were	been	ser/estar
become	became	become	tornar-se
begin	began	begun	começar
bet	bet	bet	apostar
bite	bit	bitten	morder
break	broke	broken	quebrar
bring	brought	brought	comprar
build	built	built	construir
burn	burnt / burned	burnt / burned	queimar
buy	bought	bought	comprar
catch	caught	caught	pegar
choose	chose	chosen	escolher
come	came	come	vir
cost	cost	cost	custar
cut	cut	cut	cortar
do	did	done	fazer
draw	drew	drawn	desenhar
drink	drank	drunk	beber
drive	drove	driven	dirigir
eat	ate	eaten	comer
fall	fell	fallen	cair
feed	fed	fed	alimentar
feel	felt	felt	sentir
fight	fought	fought	brigar
find	found	found	achar
fly	flew	flown	voar
forget	forgot	forgotten	esquecer
forgive	forgave	forgiven	perdoar
freeze	froze	frozen	congelar
get	got	gotten	obter
give	gave	given	dar

Irregular Verbs

Infinitive	Simple Past	Past Participle	Translation
go	went	gone	ir
grow	grew	grown	crescer
have	had	had	ter
hear	heard	heard	ouvir
hide	hid	hidden	esconder
hit	hit	hit	bater
hold	held	held	segurar
hurt	hurt	hurt	machucar
keep	kept	kept	conservar
know	knew	known	saber
lay	laid	laid	colocar
lead	led	led	guiar/liderar
learn	learnt/learned	learnt/learned	aprender
leave	left	left	partir
lend	lent	lent	emprestar
let	let	let	deixar
lie	lay	lain	deitar
light	lit	lit	acender
lose	lost	lost	perder
make	made	made	fazer
mean	meant	meant	significar
meet	met	met	encontrar
pay	paid	paid	pagar
put	put	put	colocar
read	read	read	ler
ride	rode	ridden	conduzir
ring	rang	rung	tocar
rise	rose	risen	erguer-se
run	ran	run	correr
say	said	said	dizer
see	saw	seen	ver
seek	sought	sought	procurar

Infinitive	Simple Past	Past Participle	Translation
sell	sold	sold	vender
send	sent	sent	enviar
set	set	set	estabelecer
shake	shook	shaken	balançar
shine	shone/shined	shone	brilhar
show	showed	shown	mostrar
shut	shut	shut	fechar
sing	sang	sung	cantar
sink	sank	sunk	afundar
sit	sat	sat	sentar-se
sleep	slept	slept	dormir
speak	spoke	spoken	falar
spend	spent	spent	gastar
split	split	split	dividir
spread	spread	spread	espalhar
stand	stood	stood	ficar em pé
steal	stole	stolen	roubar
swear	swore	sworn	praguejar/jurar
sweep	swept	swept	varrer
swim	swam	swum	nadar
take	took	taken	levar
teach	taught	taught	ensinar
tear	tore	torn	rasgar
tell	told	told	dizer/contar
think	thought	thought	pensar
throw	threw	thrown	arremessar
understand	understood	understood	entender
wake	woke	woken	acordar
wear	wore	worn	usar/vestir
win	won	won	ganhar
write	wrote	written	escrever

BOOKS

Dictionary

Cambridge Essential English Dictionary, by Cambridge University Press, 2004.

Longman Dictionary of Contemporary English, Pearson Education do Brasil, 2009.

Practical English Usage, by Michael Swan, Oxford: Oxford University Press, 2005.

Grammar

Collins Cobuild Student's Grammar, by Dave Willis, Harper Collins (UK), 1995.

English Grammar In Use, by Raymond Murphy, Cambridge University Press – ELT, 2004.

Grammar Express Basic, by Marjorie Fuchs and Margaret Bonner, Longman.

Practical English Usage, by Michael Swan, Oxford: Oxford University Press, 2005.

Pronunciation

Focus on Pronunciation 1 - Beginning, by Linda Lane, 2005.

Reading

American Life, by Vicky Shipton, Pearson Education, 2011.

Amistad, by D'Arcy Adrian-Vallance, Evadne Adrian-Vallance, and Joyce Annette Barnes, Pearson Education, 1999.

Baychimo - Arctic Ghost Ship, by Anthony Dalton, Heritage House, 2006.

Castaways of the Flying Dutchman, by Brian Jacques, Firebird, 2003.

Chew On This: Everything You Don't Want to Know About Fast Food, by Charles Wilson, Houghton Mifflin, 2007.

Encyclopedia Britannica – Micropaedia volume VIII, Inc. 1974, William Benton Publisher, 1943-1973, Helen Hemingway Benton, Publisher.

Eating Disorders Information for Teens: Health Tips About Anorexia, Bulimia, Binge Eating, and Other Eating Disorders (Teen Health Series), by Sandra Augustyn Lawton, Omnigraphics Inc., 2009.

Food, by Caroline Laidlaw, Pearson ELT, 2002.

Inventions That Changed the World, by David Maule, Penguin Longman Readers, 2008.

Moby Dick, Or the Whale, by Herman Melville, Simon & Brown, 2012.

My Inventions and Other Writings, by Nikola Tesla, Penguin Classics, 2011.

Round the World in Eighty Days, by Jules Verne, Barry Moser, and George Makepeace Towle, 1988.

The Phantom of the Opera, by Gaston Leroux, retold by Coleen Degnan-Veness, Penguin Readers, England, 2008.

The Pearl, by John Steinbeck, Penguin Books, 1993.

The New Way Things Work, by David Macaulay, Houghton Mifflin Books for Children, 1998.

The Story of the Middle Ages, by Samuel B. Harding, Yesterday's Classics, 2006.

Treasure Diving With Captain Dom, by Yvonne Addario, Adventure In Discovery, 2007.

United Nations (Organizations That Help the World), by Michael Pollard, Silver Burdett Pr, 1994.

Movies

A Última Hora (*The 11th Hour*, USA, 2007)

Documentário (narrado e produzido por Leonardo DiCaprio) aborda os desastres naturais causados pela própria humanidade.

Coração de Cavaleiro (*A Knight's Tale*, USA, 2001)

O filho de um pobre camponês na França do séc. XIV busca realizar seu sonho de infância: se tornar um cavaleiro.

A Lenda da Vida / O Mistério da Ilha (*The Secret of Roan Inish*, Ireland/USA, 1995)

Uma menina procura seu irmão perdido e acaba trazendo para a vida real uma fantástica e emocionante lenda irlandesa.

Os Amores de Pandora (*Pandora and the Flying Dutchman*, UK, 1951)

Uma interpretação da lenda do Holandês Voador.

A História de Ellen Hart Pena (*Dying to Be Perfect: The Ellen Hart Pena Story*, USA, 1996)

Corredora é forçada a perder peso para participar dos jogos Olímpicos e acaba vítima da anorexia nervosa.

Super Size Me - A Dieta do Palhaço (*Super Size Me*, USA, 2004)

Um documentário sobre a influência da indústria do *fast food* e as consequências em nossa saúde.

SITES

Cognates and false friends

http://www.sk.com.br/sk-fals.html

http://www.solinguainglesa.com.br/conteudo/falsos_cognatos1.php

Collocations

http://esl.fis.edu/grammar/easy/colloc.htm

http://esl.about.com/od/engilshvocabulary/a/collocations.htm

http://elc.polyu.edu.hk/advdicts/collocation.htm

Dictionary

http://dictionary.sensagent.com/perks/en-en/

www.enchantedlearning.com/dictionarysubjects/astronomy.shtml

www.ldoceonline.com/
www.merriam-webster.com/
www.morewords.com/
www.thefreedictionary.com
http://en.wiktionary.org/wiki/every
www.yourdictionary.com/

Games and exercises

http://a4esl.org/q/h/vm/raise-rise.html
www.bbc.co.uk/ (click on Learning English)
www.english-zone.com/verbs/raise.html
www.hsw.uol.com.br/quiz-list.htm
http://kids.discovery.com/games/pompeii/pompeii.html
http://languagearts.pppst.com/affixes.html

Grammar

www.edufind.com/english/grammar/
www.ego4u.com/
www.englishclub.com/grammar/
http://learnenglish.britishcouncil.org/en/quick-grammar
http://learnenglish.britishcouncil.org/en/grammar-games
http://learnenglish.britishcouncil.org/en/vocabulary-games

Idioms

http://idioms.thefreedictionary.com
www.yourdictionary.com/idioms

Indefinites and indefinite compounds

http://www.grammar-quizzes.com/agr_someany.html

Modal verbs

http://esl.fis.edu/grammar/rules/modal.htm

Phrasal verbs

http://usingenglish.com/quizzes/

Prefixes

www.english-for-students.com/Negative-Prefixes.html
www.kwiznet.com/p/takeQuiz.php?ChapterID=1174&CurriculumID=26
www.primaryresources.co.uk/english/PC_prefix2.htm

Prepositions

www.englishpage.com/prepositions/prepositions.html
http://grammar.ccc.commnet.edu/grammar/prepositions.htm

Pronunciation

www.teaching-esl-to-adults.com/english-past-tense-pronunciation.html

Question tags

http://www.englishgrammarsecrets.com/questionstags/menu.php

Relative pronouns and relative clauses

http://www.ego4u.com/en/cram-up/grammar/relative-clauses

Songs

www.lyricstime.com

Suffixes

http://dictionary.reference.com/browse/-ize?qsrc=2446
www.learnenglish.de/grammar/suffixtext.htm
www.sk.com.br/sk-morfo.html
www.usingenglish.com/glossary/suffix.html

Tests

http://www.learnenglish.de/englishtestspage.html

Verb tenses

http://www.perfect-english-grammar.com/verb-tenses.html

Writing

http://esl.about.com/ and search "writing skills"
www.wikihow.com/Write-a-Formal-Email

MISCELLANEOUS

Technology

http://www.technologyreview.com/

Massachusetts Institute of Technology

http://web.mit.edu/

Time Magazine

http://www.time.com/time/

Reader's Digest Magazine

http://www.rd.com/

Predictions

http://longbets.org/

References

Scuba Diving

www.scubadviser.com/

http://aquaviews.net/

The United Nations

http://www.un.org/

Encyclopedia Sites

http://www.britannica.com/

http://www.encyclopedia.com/

http://www.bartleby.com/

http://www.infoplease.com/encyclopedia/

http://www.questia.com/library

Medieval Life and Times

http://www.medieval-life-and-times.info/

Biographies

http://www.biography.com/

The National Eating Disorders Association

http://www.nationaleatingdisorders.org/

News

http://www.bbc.co.uk/news/

U.S. Food and Drug Administration

http://www.fda.gov/

Smithsonian Magazine

http://www.smithsonianmag.com/

Cars of the Future

http://www.sciencenewsforkids.org/2011/10/cars-of-the-future/

Flags of the World

http://www.crwflags.com/fotw/flags/

Museum of Ancient Inventions

http://www.smith.edu/hsc/museum/ancient_inventions/hsclist.htm

Brazilian Legends

http://www.oas.org/children/mitos/Brasil/Mitos.html

Food Labels

http://www.nhs.uk/Livewell/Goodfood/Pages/food-labelling.aspx#Nut

Index

Vocabulary Log